OECD Skills Studies

Building Skills for All in Australia

POLICY INSIGHTS FROM THE SURVEY OF ADULT SKILLS

This work is published under the responsibility of the Secretary-General of the OECD. The opinions expressed and arguments employed herein do not necessarily reflect the official views of OECD member countries.

This document, as well as any data and any map included herein, are without prejudice to the status of or sovereignty over any territory, to the delimitation of international frontiers and boundaries and to the name of any territory, city or area.

Please cite this publication as:
OECD (2017), *Building Skills for All in Australia: Policy Insights from the Survey of Adult Skills*, OECD Skills Studies, OECD Publishing, Paris.
http://dx.doi.org/10.1787/9789264281110-en

ISBN 978-92-64-28296-4 (print)
ISBN 978-92-64-28111-0 (PDF)

Series: OECD Skills Studies
ISSN 2307-8723 (print)
ISSN 2307-8731 (online)

The statistical data for Israel are supplied by and under the responsibility of the relevant Israeli authorities. The use of such data by the OECD is without prejudice to the status of the Golan Heights, East Jerusalem and Israeli settlements in the West Bank under the terms of international law.

Photo credits: Cover © iStockphoto.com/aleksandr-mansurov.ru/.

Corrigenda to OECD publications may be found on line at: *www.oecd.org/about/publishing/corrigenda.htm*.
© OECD 2017

You can copy, download or print OECD content for your own use, and you can include excerpts from OECD publications, databases and multimedia products in your own documents, presentations, blogs, websites and teaching materials, provided that suitable acknowledgement of OECD as source and copyright owner is given. All requests for public or commercial use and translation rights should be submitted to *rights@oecd.org*. Requests for permission to photocopy portions of this material for public or commercial use shall be addressed directly to the Copyright Clearance Center (CCC) at *info@copyright.com* or the Centre français d'exploitation du droit de copie (CFC) at *contact@cfcopies.com*.

Foreword

Not only are skills, including basic literacy and numeracy, critical to the prosperity and well-being of individuals, they are also key drivers of economic growth and societal advancement. The OECD's international Survey of Adult Skills aims to help countries secure better skills policies by measuring the basic skills of adults in 33 countries and demonstrating how these skills relate to economic and social outcomes.

This report, *Building Skills for All in Australia: Policy Insights from the Survey of Adult Skills*, explores the main strengths of the Australian skills system and areas where Australian performance could be improved. It underlines how Australia compares with other countries and what this means for policy-making.

By international standards, Australia's performance ranges from very good to average. Although these results are not poor, "average" may lead to Australia being left behind in terms of innovation and economic growth by countries that have been more successfully investing in the skills of their people. An estimated three million adult Australians are living with the consequences of low basic skills.

Skills contribute effectively to the strength of the economy. However, in the context of global upskilling and increasing competition for skills in global markets, it is important that Australia takes action. This should include strengthening focus on basic skills throughout initial schooling and in post-secondary programmes, and reaching out to disconnected youth. The report puts forward a set of eight key recommendations designed to that end.

This study is part of a series on low-skilled adults, previously conducted in the United States, England (United Kingdom) and Finland. These reports are designed to ensure that countries make the most out of their skills policies, by building on the findings from the Survey of Adult Skills both for policy development and for charting a way forward. The OECD is firmly committed to supporting countries in their bid to develop "better skills policies for better lives."

This report was drafted by Tanja Bastianić and Małgorzata Kuczera. Elisa Larrakoetxea and Jennifer Cannon provided valuable administrative support. We are very grateful to colleagues in Australia in the Department of Education and Training for their contributions to the review, in particular Ben Matheson, Emma Fleetwood, Fiona Rochford, Tracey Murphy and Fran Wylie. Patrick Donaldson from the Australian Permanent Delegation to the OECD provided helpful support in the co-ordination of the project. We are also very grateful to Gary Niedorfer from the Australian Bureau of Statistics for giving us access to the additional PIAAC data. Finally, within the OECD we would also like to thank Deborah Roseveare for her advice and support.

Table of contents

Foreword 3

Executive summary 9
    Key findings 9
    Strengths of the Australian system 9
    Policy recommendations 10

Assessment and recommendations 13
    Key findings 13
    Strengths of the Australian system 14
    Policy recommendations 14

Chapter 1. Basic skills in Australia 17
    Introduction 18
    The basic skills challenge 18
    Characteristics of the low skilled in Australia 22
    The consequences of having low skills 25
    References 29

Chapter 2. Strengths of the skills system in Australia 31
    Strength 1: Immigrants in Australia are well skilled 32
    Strength 2: Strong performance in ICT skills 35
    Strength 3: In Australia, the workplace is conducive to learning 39
    References 43

Chapter 3. Numeracy skills are not as good as literacy skills in Australia 45
    Characteristics of adults with low numeracy skills 46
    The consequences of not having good numeracy skills 51
    Recommendations: How to tackle low performance in numeracy 51
    References 55

Chapter 4. Low-skilled adults in post-secondary vocational education and training (VET) in Australia 57
    Characteristics of low-skilled post-secondary VET graduates 58
    The consequences of being a low-skilled post-secondary VET graduate 59
    Recommendations: How to address the challenge of low basic skills in post-secondary VET 62
    References 67

Chapter 5. Many young low-skilled Australians are not in employment, education or training (NEET) 69
    The NEET challenge 70
    Characteristics of NEETs 70

The consequences of being NEET 74
Recommendations: How to tackle the NEET challenge 75
References 80

Annex A. Key figures on adult skills in Australia versus other countries 81

Annex B. Problem solving in technology-rich environments – Sample items 84

Tables

Table 1.1. Academic and vocational education and training (VET) qualifications in Australia 24
Table 2.1. Low skilled in Australia use their skills in the workplace more often than their peers in other countries 42
Table 3.1. Basic skills demands of upper-secondary qualifications across countries 53

Figures

Figure 1.1. Share of adults with low basic skills 22
Figure 1.2. Mean numeracy score differences between adults with high and low-educated parents 25
Figure 1.3. Low-skilled adults are less often employed than the highly skilled 26
Figure 1.4. Low skilled out of the labour force vs. those who are employed 26
Figure 1.5. Participation rate in adult education and training (AET) 27
Figure 1.6. Numeracy proficiency and positive social outcomes 28
Figure 2.1. Share of low-skilled adults among immigrants and natives, by age 32
Figure 2.2. Share of adults with tertiary education, by immigrant background 34
Figure 2.3. Labour force participation by immigrant background 35
Figure 2.4. Proficiency in problem solving in technology-rich environments 37
Figure 2.5. Share of adults scoring at Level 2 or 3 in PSTRE, by age group 37
Figure 2.6. How often low-skilled workers learn work-related skills from co-workers and supervisors .. 41
Figure 3.1. Literacy and numeracy skills, by levels 47
Figure 3.2. Performance of immigrants in numeracy and literacy 48
Figure 3.3. Performance of young people in PISA and in PIAAC 50
Figure 4.1. Low skilled among post-secondary VET graduates 58
Figure 4.2. Skills distribution among current students 60
Figure 4.3. Employment rates among post-secondary VET graduates 60
Figure 4.4. Effect of skills on earnings of post-secondary VET graduates 61
Figure 5.1. Young people with low skills are more likely to become NEET 71
Figure 5.2. Are those with less educated parents more likely to become NEET? 72
Figure 5.3. Non-NEET youth score higher for non-cognitive abilities than NEETs 73
Figure 5.4. Share of NEET among native born and immigrants 73
Figure 5.5. NEET costs are significant in many OECD countries 75

Figure A A.1. Literacy proficiency and positive social outcomes 81
Figure A A.2. Percentage of first and second-generation migrants that have low basic skills (below Level 2 in literacy or/and numeracy) in comparison with the native-born 82
Figure A A.3. Students and recently graduated students from post-secondary VET who lack basic skills 82
Figure A A.4. In which sectors do post-secondary VET graduates work? 83

Boxes

Box 1.1. The OECD Survey of Adult Skills 19
Box 1.2. How low basic skills are measured in the Survey of Adult Skills (PIAAC) 20
Box 2.1. Organised on-the-job training attended in the last 12 months 39
Box 3.1. Inspiring the Future: Career guidance and gender 52
Box 3.2. Reform of the school system in England (United Kingdom) 54
Box 4.1. How the United States responded to the quality challenge in post-secondary VET 63
Box 4.2. Innovative initiatives addressing poor basic skills in colleges in the United States 65
Box 5.1. The definition of NEET used in this report 70
Box 5.2. How to increase completion 76

Follow OECD Publications on:

 http://twitter.com/OECD_Pubs

 http://www.facebook.com/OECDPublications

 http://www.linkedin.com/groups/OECD-Publications-4645871

 http://www.youtube.com/oecdilibrary

 http://www.oecd.org/oecddirect/

This book has...
A service that delivers Excel® files from the printed page!

Look for the *StatLinks* at the bottom of the tables or graphs in this book. To download the matching Excel® spreadsheet, just type the link into your Internet browser, starting with the *http://dx.doi.org* prefix, or click on the link from the e-book edition.

Executive summary

Key findings

Australia's overall performance in the PIAAC Survey of Adult Skills, which is a product of the OECD Programme for the International Assessment of Adult Competencies (PIAAC), across literacy, numeracy and problem solving in technology-rich environments ranges from average to very good.

However, one in five Australians – around three million adults – have low literacy and/or numeracy skills, according to the PIAAC Survey of Adult Skills, which was conducted in Australia from October 2011 to March 2012. For the purposes of this report, adults with low literacy or numeracy skills are not able to reach Level 2 proficiency in literacy or numeracy on a scale that goes up to Level 5.

Australia has a similar share of adults with low literacy and/or numeracy skills as New Zealand. It has a smaller proportion of adults with low skills than the United States, the United Kingdom (England and Northern Ireland) and most European Mediterranean countries but a larger share than Nordic countries, Japan, and the Netherlands.

Taken together, although Australia's average results are not poor, the challenges presented by adults with low basic skills may lead to Australia being left behind in terms of innovation and economic growth by countries that have been more successfully investing in the skills of all their people.

A closer examination of Australia's performance reveals the following:

- Numeracy represents a particular challenge in Australia.
- Signs of poor numeracy performance can be traced back to initial schooling.
- Women have weaker numeracy skills than men.
- There is a relatively large gap between the most proficient and least proficient adults in literacy and in numeracy.
- Many well-educated adults have low literacy and/or numeracy skills.
- Young women in Australia are much more likely to be not in employment, education or training (NEET) than young men.

Strengths of the Australian system

While the OECD Survey of Adult Skills (PIAAC) shows that Australia needs to strengthen some aspects of its skills system to achieve better outcomes, the results also show that the Australian skills system has strengths that the country can build on.

Many migrants are well educated and highly skilled

Australia has a large population of well-skilled and well-educated migrants, many of whom are young. These skilled migrants bring highly attractive and much-needed skills to the workforce. Migrants in Australia generally integrate successfully into the mainstream society, as measured by their labour market outcomes and the basic skills of their offspring.

Computer and ICT skills are strong

By international standards, adults in Australia, across all age groups, have strong skills in problem solving in technology-rich environments. This is important as adults who are not familiar with computers will be poorly equipped to respond to new work requirements spurred by new technology.

Workplaces contribute to stronger skills

In Australia, jobs provide more learning opportunities, including for those with low skills, than jobs in many other countries. The workplace is therefore an important and strong element of the skills system in Australia.

Policy recommendations

While this report discusses how to improve basic skills in adult population, it should be recognised that underperformance on basic skills can be traced back to earlier stages of education. For example, poor performance of the post-secondary vocational education and training (VET) system very likely reflects a selection effect whereby those with lower basic skills are more likely to enter VET pathways. Australia could achieve better economic and social outcomes by tackling the challenges of how to improve numeracy skills, how to ensure that post-secondary VET programmes lead to strong basic skills, and how to address the issue of young NEET adults, many of whom are low skilled. The policy recommendations listed below are designed to respond to these challenges.

Increase participation of women in STEM fields by breaking down gender stereotypes and encouraging women to enter these fields.

Young women often do not translate their good school performance into choosing a field of study that offers better employment prospects, such as studies in science, technology, engineering and mathematics (STEM) fields. To increase participation of women in STEM fields Australia has recently introduced the National Innovation and Science Agenda (www.innovation.gov.au).

Strengthen the focus on mathematics throughout secondary education.

International comparison shows that while young adults in Australia have strong literacy skills, in numeracy they lag behind their peers with comparable qualifications. The Australian Government recently introduced several initiatives to tackle this issue.

Identify students in post-secondary VET who are at risk of low basic skills and provide targeted initiatives to support them.

Post-secondary VET students whose highest qualification is below upper-secondary or upper-secondary VET are much more likely to perform poorly in basic skills than their peers with higher levels of education. Women are also over-represented among students with low basic numeracy and literacy skills. These findings show that initiatives targeting specific categories of post-secondary VET students could be particularly effective.

Ensure that literacy and numeracy skills are part of the quality criteria in post-secondary VET.

Some institutions may accept students with poor basic skills with no intention or capacity to address this challenge. Basic numeracy and literacy should therefore underpin all post-secondary VET qualifications.

Encourage post-secondary VET providers to address weak literacy and numeracy skills.

Remediating poor literacy and numeracy skills is difficult, but not impossible. Providers of post-secondary VET qualifications should be encouraged to address underperformance in these basic skills more vigorously and effectively.

Reach out to disconnected youth and prevent dropout at earlier stages of education.

Typically, students who are at risk of dropping out early from school disengage gradually, and there are early signs that can be helpful in identifying these students.

Use pre-apprenticeships to help NEETs re-enter education and training, and to find employment.

Various initiatives that facilitate the transition from joblessness to training, or that provide a bridge between schools and apprenticeships, can be used to better prepare young people for their apprenticeship.

Improve access to childcare facilities for young mothers.

In order to help NEETs with children, particularly women, to enter the labour market or facilitate a return to education and training, childcare should be easily accessible and costs should be kept at an affordable level.

Assessment and recommendations

Key findings

Australia's overall performance in the PIAAC Survey of Adult Skills across literacy, numeracy and problem solving in technology-rich environments ranges from average to very good.

However, one in five Australians – around three million adults – have low literacy and/or numeracy skills, according to the PIAAC Survey of Adult Skills, which was conducted in Australia from October 2011 to March 2012. For the purposes of this report, adults with low literacy or numeracy skills are not able to reach Level 2 proficiency in literacy or numeracy on a scale that goes up to Level 5.

Australia has a similar share of adults with low literacy and/or numeracy skills as New Zealand. It has a smaller proportion of adults with low skills than the United States, the United Kingdom (England and Northern Ireland) and most European Mediterranean countries but a larger share than Nordic countries, Japan, and the Netherlands.

Numeracy represents a particular challenge in Australia. Around 93% of Australian adults with low literacy and/or numeracy skills perform poorly in numeracy. However, around 42% of adults with low skills can reach at least Level 2 in literacy. In contrast, only 7% of adults have low literacy skills but reach at least Level 2 in numeracy.

Taken together, although Australia's average results are not poor, the challenges presented by adults with low basic skills may lead to Australia being left behind in terms of innovation and economic growth by countries that have been more successfully investing in the skills of all their people.

A closer examination of Australia's performance reveals the following:

- There is a relatively large gap between the most proficient and least proficient adults in literacy and in numeracy.
- Many well-educated adults have low literacy and/or numeracy skills. Around 30% of low skilled adults have completed education at upper secondary level and around 20% beyond upper-secondary level.
- Signs of poor numeracy performance can be traced back to initial schooling. The Programme for International Student Assessment (PISA) a triennial evaluation that tests the basic skills of 15-year-olds, shows the numeracy skills of young people in Australia continuously decreased between 2003 and 2012. The PISA study also shows that Australia has a larger skills gap among 15-year-olds (as measured by the difference between the 5th and 95th percentiles) than many other OECD countries.
- Women have weaker numeracy skills than men. Women are also less likely to study in the fields of study that require strong mathematical skills, such as science, technology, engineering and mathematics (STEM) fields.

- Young women in Australia are much more likely to be not in employment, education or training (NEET) than young men. Gender is more strongly associated with NEET status in Australia than in all other countries, except Turkey. Speaking a language other than English and leaving education and training early are also risk factors of being a NEET in Australia.

Strengths of the Australian system

While the PIAAC Survey of Adult Skills shows that Australia needs to strengthen some aspects of its skills system to achieve better outcomes, the results also show that the Australian skills system has strengths that the country can build on.

Many migrants are well educated and highly skilled

Australia has a large population of well-skilled and well-educated migrants, many of whom are young. These skilled migrants bring highly attractive and much-needed skills to the workforce.

Migrants in Australia generally integrate successfully into the mainstream society, as measured by their labour market outcomes and the basic skills of their offspring. Migrants in Australia are also more likely to work in skilled and well-paid jobs compared to migrants in other countries. And in contrast to many other countries, second-generation migrants have literacy and numeracy skills comparable to those of natives.

These positive outcomes can be explained by migration policy in Australia, which gives priority to skilled migrants and successfully supports integration of newcomers into mainstream society.

Computer and ICT skills are strong

By international standards, adults in Australia, across all age groups, have strong skills in problem solving in technology-rich environments. This is important as ICT technologies and the use of computers have changed working methods and work organisation. Employment in jobs subject to automation has been shrinking, along with the demand for the skills necessary to perform these jobs. These trends could accelerate in the future as technology is increasingly applied in workplaces, and computers are able to perform more and more complex tasks. Adults who are not familiar with computers will therefore be poorly equipped to respond to new work requirements spurred by new technology.

Workplaces contribute to stronger skills

People develop their skills in the workplace, through formalised training, daily interactions with colleagues and supervisors and simply by doing their work. In Australia, jobs provide more learning opportunities, including for those with low skills, than jobs in many other countries. The workplace is therefore an important and strong element of the skills system in Australia. Drawing on this positive experience, Australia could promote and scale up work arrangements and management practices that lead to the best outcomes in terms of skills improvement.

Policy recommendations

Australia could achieve better economic and social outcomes by tackling the challenges of how to improve numeracy skills, how to ensure that post-secondary vocational education and training (VET) leads to strong basic skills, and how to address the issue of young NEET adults, many of whom are low skilled. The policy recommendations listed below are designed to respond to these challenges. While this report discusses how to improve basic skills in adult population, it should be recognised that underperformance on basic skills can be traced back to earlier stages of education. For example, poor performance of the post-secondary VET system very likely reflects a selection effect whereby those with lower basic skills are more likely to enter VET pathways. It means the observed skills gap among adults should not be squarely attributed to poor performance of the VET system. That does not diminish the importance of addressing poor skills through the VET system, if that is where the problem is concentrated.

1. Increase participation of women in STEM fields by breaking down gender stereotypes and encouraging women to enter these fields.

   Gender differences in educational choices are often related to student attitudes (motivation, interest) in studying a particular subject, rather than their ability and school performance. Young women often do not translate their good school performance into choosing a field of study that offers better employment prospects, such as studies in STEM fields. As well as the social and economic benefits, policies to attract and retain more women in the STEM workforce would help reduce occupational segmentation in the labour force and improve gender equity in labour market outcomes. To increase participation of women in STEM fields Australia has recently introduced the National Innovation and Science Agenda (www.innovation.gov.au).

2. Strengthen the focus on mathematics throughout secondary education.

   International comparison shows that while young adults in Australia have strong literacy skills, in numeracy they lag behind their peers with comparable qualifications. While this finding cannot be directly connected to the design of the school system in Australia, it raises questions regarding the effectiveness of the school system in developing strong numeracy skills in young people. The Australian Government recently introduced several initiatives to tackle this issue.

3. Identify students in post-secondary VET who are at risk of low basic skills and provide targeted initiatives to support them.

   Australian post-secondary VET is inclusive and caters to a very diverse population. While this is a strength, it can be challenging to address the needs of a very diverse population. Post-secondary VET students whose highest qualification is below upper-secondary or upper-secondary VET are much more likely to perform poorly in basic skills than their peers with higher levels of education. Women are also over-represented among students with low basic numeracy and literacy skills. These findings show that initiatives targeting specific categories of post-secondary VET students, such as those with low VET qualifications and students in specific fields of study, could be particularly effective.

4. Ensure that literacy and numeracy skills are part of the quality criteria in post-secondary VET.

   Recent reforms established a market in the provision of post-secondary VET, with public and private providers competing for public money. These reforms aimed to increase the number of VET participants, improve access to post-secondary education, and boost student choice. However, the reforms also created a system that is complex and difficult to understand for students, and where quality varies largely across providers. Some institutions may accept students with poor basic skills with no intention or capacity to address this challenge. Basic numeracy and literacy should therefore underpin all post-secondary VET qualifications.

5. Encourage post-secondary VET providers to address weak literacy and numeracy skills.

   Remediating poor literacy and numeracy skills is difficult, but not impossible. Providers of post-secondary VET qualifications should be encouraged to address underperformance in these basic skills more vigorously and effectively.

6. Reach out to disconnected youth and prevent dropout at earlier stages of education.

   Reaching out to young people at risk who are still in school is easier than targeting those who have already left and are loosely connected to the labour market. Young people who leave education and training early are more likely to become NEET. Typically, students who are at risk of dropping out early from school disengage gradually, and there are early signs that can be helpful in identifying these students.

7. Use pre-apprenticeships to help NEETs re-enter education and training, and to find employment.

   Apprenticeships, or traineeships, can be a powerful tool to engage disconnected youth as they offer an opportunity to learn and connect to the world of work. However, finding and successfully completing an apprenticeship may be particularly difficult for those most in need. Various initiatives that facilitate the transition from joblessness to training, or that provide a bridge between schools and apprenticeships, can be used to better prepare young people for their apprenticeship.

8. Improve access to childcare facilities for young mothers.

   Young women in Australia are much more likely to become NEET than young men. In Australia, this association is one of the highest among countries participating in the Survey of Adult Skills, which signals the level of importance of the problem. In order to help NEETs with children, particularly women, to enter the labour market or facilitate a return to education and training, childcare should be easily accessible and costs should be kept at an affordable level.

Chapter 1. Basic skills in Australia

In Australia an estimated three million adults have low basic skills according to the OECD Survey of Adult Skills (PIAAC). Relative to other OECD countries in the Survey, adults in Australia have an above-average performance in literacy, but only average numeracy skills. Well-developed literacy and numeracy skills have a positive impact on economic and social development for both individuals and societies. This chapter describes the characteristics of the low skilled in Australia, and discusses the consequences that low skills have on their economic and social outcomes. As in most OECD countries, the low skilled in Australia are more likely to be inactive, earn less, work in elementary occupations and report low levels of well-being.

The statistical data for Israel are supplied by and are under the responsibility of the relevant Israeli authorities. The use of such data by the OECD is without prejudice to the status of the Golan Heights, East Jerusalem and Israeli settlements in the West Bank under the terms of international law.

Introduction

Building Skills for All: An overview

This study on Australia, *Building Skills for All: Policy Insights from the Survey of Adult Skills*, is part of a series on low-skilled adults. It draws on findings from the Survey of Adult Skills, which is a product of the OECD Programme for the International Assessment of Adult Competencies (PIAAC) (see Box 1.1). A similar study was also conducted in the United States (OECD, 2013a). Full reviews involving missions to countries and a thorough analysis of the country policies bearing on skills development were carried out in England (United Kingdom) (Kuczera, Field and Windisch, 2016) and Finland (Musset, 2015).

Scope of the study

Drawing on international comparison, and in agreement with the Australian Government, this study focuses on the strengths of the Australian skills system and areas where Australian performance could be improved. It also looks at the factors promoting or limiting basic skills and what could be done through education, training or workplace measures to enhance basic skills.

How the study is structured

Chapter 1 describes who the low-skilled adults are and discusses risks associated with being a low-skilled adult in Australia. Chapter 2 focuses on the strengths of the Australian skills system. It points to strong basic skills in the migrant population, widespread knowledge of ICT in Australian society, and to the positive role of workplaces in skills development. The last three chapters focus on challenges faced by Australia in the area of basic skills, and provide policy suggestions to address these challenges. Chapter 3 discusses lower numeracy skills; Chapter 4 looks at young people who are NEET; and Chapter 5 focuses on low skills in post-secondary vocational education and training.

The basic skills challenge

How the low skilled are defined in this report

In this report "low skilled" are defined as those who are below Level 2 in literacy or numeracy in PIAAC. Problem solving in technology-rich environments (PSTRE) will be addressed separately in Chapter 2. "Adults with higher skills" refer to adults with literacy and numeracy at Level 2 and above.

Instead of using "levels of proficiency", it is sometimes more relevant to look directly at proficiency in literacy or numeracy, for example, when an association between wages and basic skills is explored. Whenever analysis is performed on individual domains, the results are reported for literacy and numeracy. As literacy and numeracy are highly correlated, those with strong skills in one domain also tend to perform well in the other.

> **Box 1.1. The OECD Survey of Adult Skills**
>
> The Survey, a product of the Programme for the International Assessment of Adult Competencies (PIAAC), assesses adult proficiency in three key information-processing skills.
>
> - **Literacy** assessment covers a range of skills, from the decoding of written words and sentences to the comprehension, interpretation and evaluation of complex texts (but not writing).
>
> - **Numeracy** assessment involves managing a situation or solving a problem in a real context by responding to mathematical content/information/ideas represented in multiple ways.
>
> - **Problem solving in technology-rich environments** assessment focuses on the ability to solve problems for personal, work and civic purposes by setting up appropriate goals, and accessing and making use of information through computers.
>
> Each of the three assessments yield results scaled from 0 to 500 points. The scales are divided into six levels in literacy and numeracy (Levels 1 to 5, plus below Level 1), and four for problem solving in technology-rich environments (Levels 1 to 3, plus below Level 1). The purpose of skills levels is to facilitate the interpretation of the results, and not to use as standards that define levels of skill required for particular purposes.
>
> The Survey also provides a rich array of information regarding respondents' use of skills at work and in everyday life, their education, their linguistic and social backgrounds, their participation in the labour market, and other aspects of their well-being.
>
> The Survey was conducted over two rounds of data collection, one in 2011-2012 and one in 2014-2015. In the first round, more than 160 000 adults aged 16 to 65 were surveyed in 24 countries and in the second round, an additional 9 countries and more than 50 000 adults were surveyed.
>
> The Survey of Adult Skills was conducted in Australia from October 2011 to March 2012. A total of 7 430 adults aged 16-65 were surveyed.
>
> *Source*: OECD (2013), *OECD Skills Outlook 2013: First Results from the Survey of Adult Skills*, http://dx.doi.org/10.1787/9789264204256-en; OECD (2013), *The Survey of Adult Skills: Reader's Companion*, http://dx.doi.org/10.1787/9789264204027-en.

What does it mean to have low skills?

"Low skills" is an abstract notion, particularly when it depends on an arbitrary cut-off point. Box 1.2 therefore gives examples of the instruments used to test whether individuals are at or below Level 2. The skills measured are those of everyday life, such as reading a petrol gauge and understanding how to sensibly take painkillers. Numeracy skills do not require specific technical capacities such as algebra, but they are mediated by literacy.

> **Box 1.2. How low basic skills are measured in the Survey of Adult Skills (PIAAC)**
>
> Individuals are classified at different levels of numeracy and literacy based on their probability of responding to tasks of different difficulty levels (see Chapter 18 in OECD, 2013b). At each point of the scale, an individual with a score of that particular value has a 67% chance of successfully completing items located at that point. Low skilled (below Level 2 with our definition) adults would, more often than not, be unable to perform these tasks.
>
> **Literacy Level 2/3**
>
>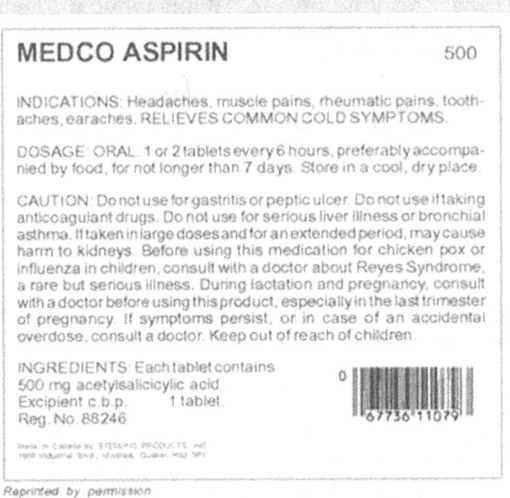
>
> Q: What is the maximum number of days you should take this medicine? List three situations for which you should consult a doctor.
>
> **Numeracy Level 2**
>
>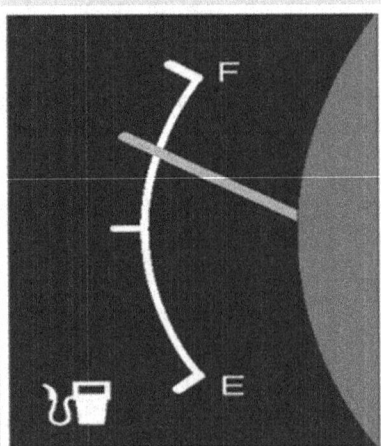
>
> Q: The petrol tank in this truck holds 48 gallons. About how many gallons of petrol remain in the tank? (Assume the gauge is accurate.).
>
> *Source*: Kuczera M., S. Field and H. Windisch (2016), *Building Skills for All: A Review of England. Policy Insights from the Survey of Adult Skills*, www.oecd.org/edu/skills-beyond-school/building-skills-for-all-review-of-england.pdf.

Skills not reported in the survey

The Survey of Adult Skills measures only a specific set of skills. Other skills, such as vocational and soft skills, are also valued in the labour market and by society and should be part of the "skills package" developed by education and training systems.

In Australia, an estimated three million 16-65 year-olds have low basic skills

According to the findings from the Survey of Adult Skills, one in five working age adults has low literacy or numeracy skills, or both. Australia has a similar share of low-skilled adults as New Zealand; a smaller proportion than the United States, the United Kingdom (England and Northern Ireland) and most European Mediterranean countries; and a larger share than Nordic countries, Japan, and the Netherlands (see Figure 1.1. Share of adults with low basic skills).

Numeracy represents a major challenge in Australia. By international standards, adults in Australia have an above-average performance in literacy, but only average numeracy skills. Low numeracy skills will be discussed in more detail in Chapter 3.

In Australia three million adults have either low numeracy or literacy skills, or both. In this group:

- A very small percentage of people have low literacy and good numeracy skills.
- More than 1 million adults have low numeracy levels and average to good literacy skills.
- 1.7 million Australians have both low numeracy and low literacy skills.

Basic skills are fundamental to life chances

Well-developed literacy and numeracy skills have a positive impact on economic and social development for both individuals and societies. Many people with weak basic skills are disadvantaged, often because they have low pay, unpleasant or insecure jobs, are unemployed, or are poor and excluded from the labour market (see for example Vignoles, Coulon, and Marcenaro-Gutierrez, 2010; Bostock and Steptoe, 2012). Policy options to address low basic skills should consider that these skills and poor life chances reinforce each other. Low basic skills lead to bad jobs, and bad jobs provide few opportunities to use and develop skills, which also contributes to skills decline.

ICT and the use of computers have revolutionised working methods and work organisation. As a result, employment in jobs subject to automation has been shrinking, along with demand for the skills necessary to perform these jobs (Acemoglu and Autor, 2011). This trend could even accelerate in the future as technology is increasingly applied in workplaces, and computers are able to perform more and more complex tasks. Sound basic skills could therefore be even more important in the future to preserve jobs and secure good life chances.

Figure 1.1. Share of adults with low basic skills

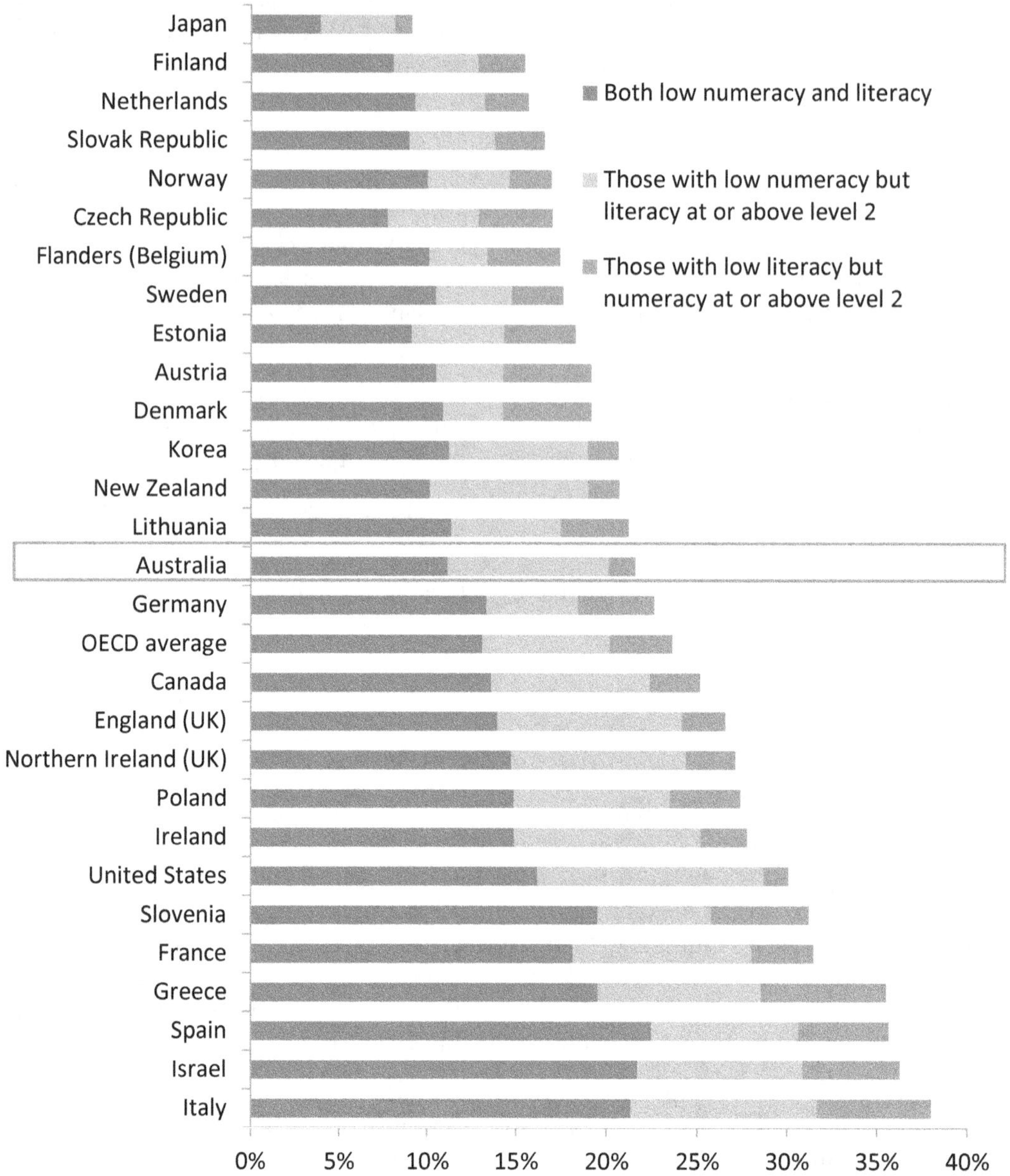

- Both low numeracy and literacy
- Those with low numeracy but literacy at or above level 2
- Those with low literacy but numeracy at or above level 2

Japan
Finland
Netherlands
Slovak Republic
Norway
Czech Republic
Flanders (Belgium)
Sweden
Estonia
Austria
Denmark
Korea
New Zealand
Lithuania
Australia
Germany
OECD average
Canada
England (UK)
Northern Ireland (UK)
Poland
Ireland
United States
Slovenia
France
Greece
Spain
Israel
Italy

Source: OECD calculations based on OECD (2016a), *Survey of Adult Skills (PIAAC)* (Database 2012, 2015), www.oecd.org/site/piaac/publicdataandanalysis.htm.

StatLink ᕹ http://dx.doi.org/10.1787/888933573259

Characteristics of the low skilled in Australia

More low skilled among older adults

In the majority of participating countries, Australia included, young people aged 16-24 score higher on literacy and numeracy scales than adults aged 55-65 (OECD, 2016, Figure 3.7). In some countries, such as Finland, Belgium (Flemish Community), France, Korea, the Netherlands, Poland and Spain, the reduction in the share of adults with low skills across generations was larger than in Australia. Differences in skills between generations can be due to the decline in skills over time, whereby skills peak around the age of 25 and then tend to decrease (see for example Paccagnella, 2016). In Australia work practices are more favourable to skills preservation than the work environment in other countries, which may explain a relatively good performance of older adults (this issue will be discussed in more detail in Chapter 2). But the skills gap between the young and older can also be explained by differences across cohorts, changes over time in education and training systems, and changes in labour market and economic and social contexts. For example, in many countries, the basic skills of young adults have improved (at least partly) due to greater availability of good quality education. Similarly in Australia, the better performance of young people can be explained, to some extent, by the fact that they are better educated and have a more favourable socio-economic status than older cohorts.

Women perform lower than men in numeracy

In Australia, men (51%) and women (49%) are equally represented among adults with low literacy, similar to many other participating countries. However, women are over-represented among those with low numeracy: 57% of women score below Level 2 compared to 43% of men. This issue is discussed in Chapter 3.

Some low-skilled adults are well educated

Table 1.1 explains how levels of educational attainment in Australia are identified in this report and how they compare to the International Standard Classification of Education (ISCED). (This classification is created for the purpose of this study and does not take into account the problems of mapping the AQF to ISCED definitions of upper-secondary and tertiary as presented in the 2009 AQF Pathways Project Technical Report (Australian Qualifications Framework Council, 2009).

Educational attainment is associated with skills levels. In Australia, nearly half of those with low skills, more than 1.3 million adults, have education and training at the level below upper-secondary (primary school, junior secondary school or certificate I, II). Many adults with low skills are well educated: around 30% of low-skilled adults have upper-secondary education (certificate III or senior secondary school), and 13% have post-secondary non-tertiary education (certificate IV, diploma, advanced diploma and associate degree). The low skilled in post-secondary education is addressed in more detail in Chapter 4. Some 9% of low-skilled adults in Australia have a tertiary degree (bachelor's degree, graduate certificate and graduate diploma, master's degree or doctoral degree).

Table 1.1. Academic and vocational education and training (VET) qualifications in Australia

	Below upper secondary	Upper secondary	Post-secondary	Tertiary
VET	ISCED 1,2 and 3C shorter than 2 years – primary school, junior secondary school or cert certificate I,II	ISCED 3C 2 years and more – certificate III	ISCED 4A-B-C and 5B and area of study – Certificate IV + Diploma, Advanced diploma and Associate Degree in the following areas of study: social science, business and law; science, mathematics and computing; teacher training and education science; engineering, manufacturing and construction; agriculture and veterinary; health and welfare; services.	
Academic		ISCED 3A-B – senior secondary School	ISCED 4A-B-C and 5B and area of study – Certificate IV + diploma, advanced diploma and associate degree in the following areas of study: general programmes, and humanities, languages and arts.	ISCED 5A and 6 – bachelor degree, graduate certificate and graduate diploma Master degree level Doctoral degree level

Low-skilled adults come from more disadvantaged backgrounds

Family background has a strong impact on skills in all countries, and in some, such as the United States, Germany and the United Kingdom, this association is particularly strong. In Australia, similar to Japan, New Zealand, the Netherlands and Nordic countries, the association between a country's average literacy and numeracy skills and parental background (measured by parental education) is weaker than in OECD countries on average.

The association between family background and skills is higher for young adults

The relationship between parents' education and skills proficiency varies across generations. In most countries, Australia included, the relationship between family background and skills proficiency is stronger among younger than older adults. For example, access to school may be closely related to social background, while subsequent skills development may primarily reflect an individual's ability, irrespective of social background. In some countries, such as the United States, Spain or Korea, the reverse is true: family background has a stronger impact on skills among older adults than younger adults.

Figure 1.2. Mean numeracy score differences between adults with high and low educated parents

At least one parent attained tertiary minus neither parent attained upper secondary, 2012 and 2015

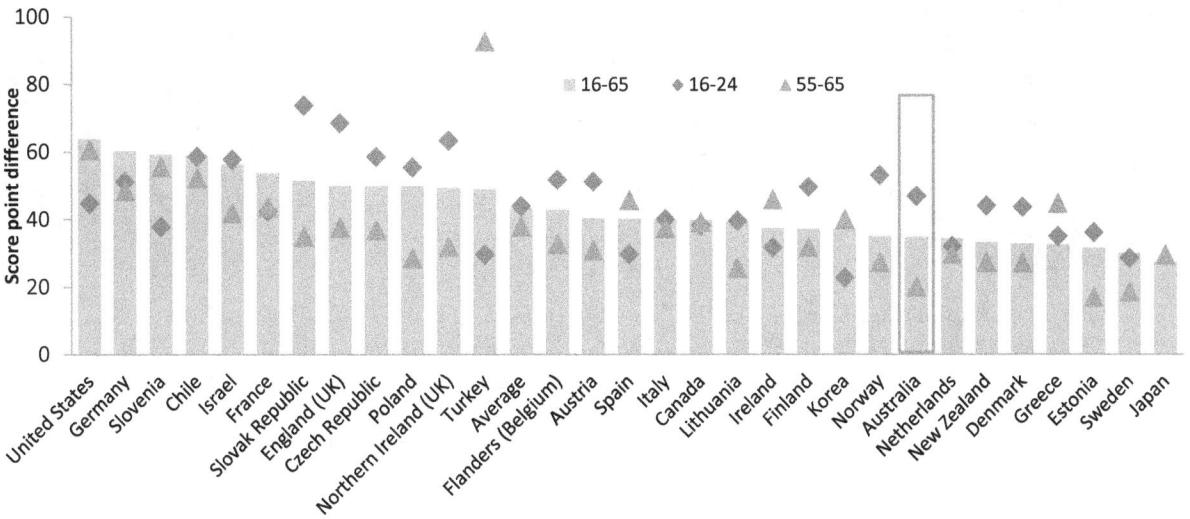

Source: OECD calculations based on OECD (2016a), *Survey of Adult Skills (PIAAC)* (Database 2012, 2015), www.oecd.org/site/piaac/publicdataandanalysis.htm.

StatLink http://dx.doi.org/10.1787/888933573278

Immigrants (foreign born) in Australia have lower skill levels than natives (native born), but better than migrants in other participating countries

The Survey of Adult Skills suggests that Australia has the highest proportion of immigrants among the participating countries. Immigrants in Australia have lower levels of literacy and numeracy than native Australians, but the difference is among the lowest across participating countries. Immigrants in Australia have better skills than immigrants in other countries. This topic is discussed in more detail in Chapter 2.

There are large difference across regions

The highest share of low-skilled adults is in Tasmania (24%) followed by the Northern Territory and Victoria; the Australian Capital Territory has the smallest share of low-skilled adults (14%).

The consequences of having low skills

Low-skilled adults are more likely to be inactive

Low-skilled adults are more likely to be out of the labour force than those with stronger basic skills. In Australia, some 60%, or two million adults, with low skills are employed, 5% of low-skilled adults are unemployed, and another 36%, or more than one million, are out of the labour force (see Figure 1.3 and Figure 1.4).

Figure 1.3. Low-skilled adults are less often employed than the highly skilled

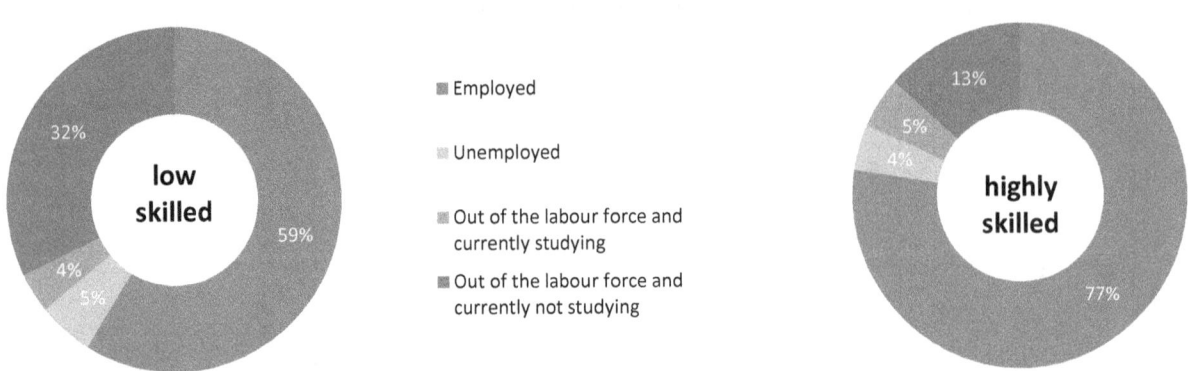

Source: OECD calculations based on OECD (2016a), *Survey of Adult Skills (PIAAC)* (Database 2012, 2015), www.oecd.org/site/piaac/publicdataandanalysis.htm.

StatLink http://dx.doi.org/10.1787/888933573297

Figure 1.4. Low skilled out of the labour force vs. those who are employed

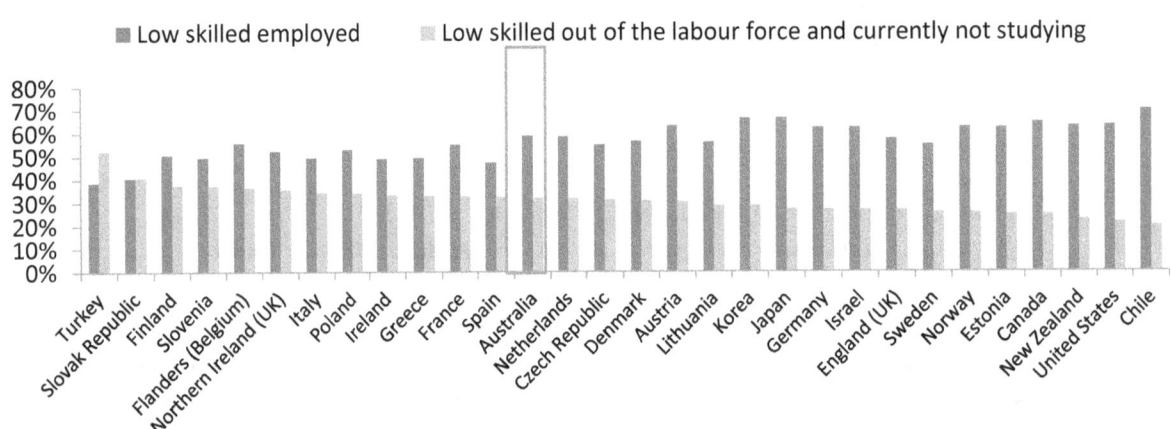

Source: OECD calculations based on OECD (2016a), *Survey of Adult Skills (PIAAC)* (Database 2012, 2015), www.oecd.org/site/piaac/publicdataandanalysis.htm.

StatLink http://dx.doi.org/10.1787/888933573316

Low-skilled adults are more likely to work in elementary occupations

Low-skilled adults are over-represented in sectors such as manufacturing and construction. Some 17%, or around 400 000 of low-skilled adults, work in elementary occupations, such as labourers and production workers relying on low basic skills, compared to 8% of adults with stronger performance. At the same time, 20% of low-skilled Australians work in skilled occupations, such as professionals and technicians. This may be because they have other skills not measured in the Survey but required in these occupations (e.g. skills in art, strong soft skills). However, such a large number of low-skilled adults in occupations requiring a high level of basic skills could also be a sign of mismatch.

Low-skilled adults earn less

Wages are strongly associated with basic skills. On average across OECD countries that participated in the survey, the median hourly wage of salaried employees with high numeracy skills (Level 4 or 5) is around 60% higher than that of workers with low numeracy skills. The same is valid for literacy skills. In Australia, this difference is even higher than in most other participating countries, and highly skilled adults earn more than those with low-skill levels. This association remains strong even when other factors, such as age, gender, immigrant status and job experience, are taken into account (OECD, 2016: 126).

Low-skilled adults are less likely to participate in adult education and training

Adults in Australia, including those with low skills, are more likely to continue in education and training after leaving formal education than their peers in other countries. However, in Australia, adults with low basic skills participate less often in adult education and training than highly proficient adults. The gap in participation rates between low and highly skilled adults is 27 percentage points (35% and 61% among low and highly skilled respectively), which is above the OECD average. Part of this difference can be explained by the job characteristics of low-skilled individuals. For example, low-skilled adults are typically in jobs that provide fewer training opportunities (Grotlüschen et al., 2016).

Figure 1.5. Participation rate in adult education and training (AET)

Participating rates for low skilled and difference in participation among low skilled and high skilled

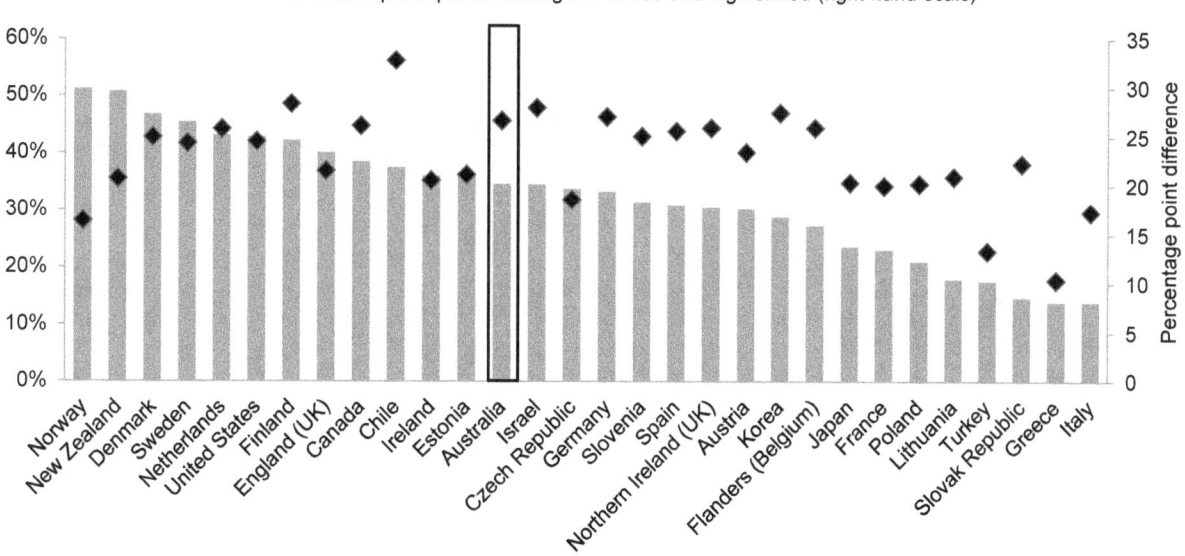

Source: OECD calculations based on OECD (2016a), *Survey of Adult Skills (PIAAC)* (Database 2012, 2015), www.oecd.org/site/piaac/publicdataandanalysis.htm.

StatLink http://dx.doi.org/10.1787/888933573335

Those with low skills report low levels of well-being

The Survey of Adult Skills collected information on four dimensions of well-being: the level of trust in others, political efficacy or the sense of influence on the political process, volunteering, and self-assessed health status. People with low levels of skills have poorer health, trust others less and are less likely to engage in community life and democratic processes than highly-skilled adults. Skill levels have a significant positive relationship with all four dimensions of well-being, even when other factors, such as gender, age, immigration background, socio-economic background and education, are taken into account. In Australia, more than in many other countries, more adults with low numeracy skills report that they do not trust others and do not participate in volunteer activities compared to highly numerate adults (Level 4/5). Highly skilled Australians, as New Zealanders and Norwegians, report much higher levels of political efficacy than their low-skilled peers. There is also an association between low skills and health in Australia, but it is slightly weaker than in many other countries. (See Figure 1.6 for an association with numeracy skills and Figure A A.1 in Annex A for an association with literacy skills).

Figure 1.6. Numeracy proficiency and positive social outcomes

Adjusted difference between the percentage of adults with high proficiency (Levels 4 and 5) and the percentage of adults with low proficiency who reported high levels of trust and political efficacy, good to excellent health, or participating in volunteer activities

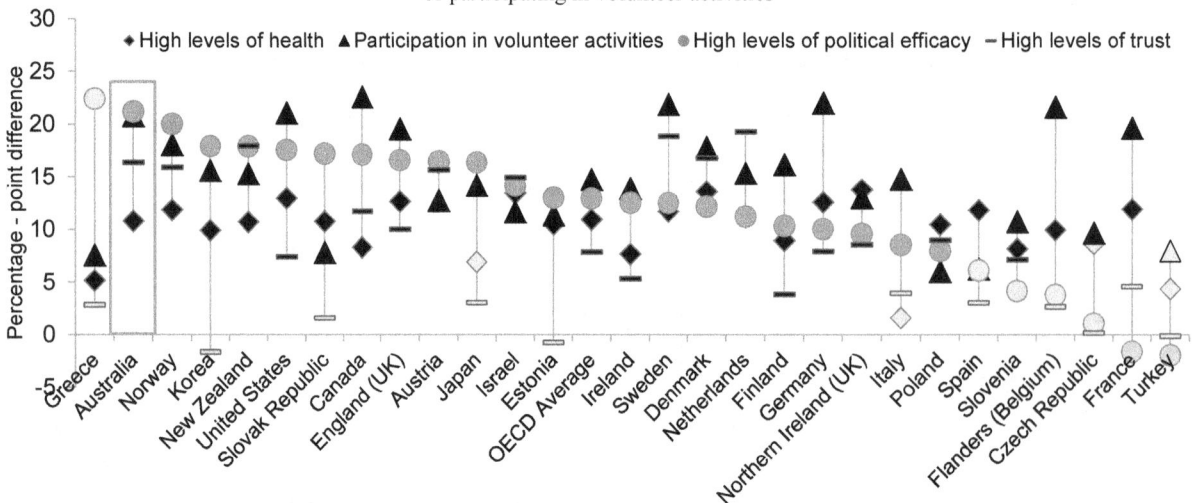

Notes: Statistically significant differences are marked in a darker tone. Adjusted differences are based on a regression model and take account of differences associated with the following variables: age, gender, education, immigrant and language background and parents' educational attainment.
Source: Adapted from OECD (2016), *Skills Matter: Further Results from the Survey of Adult Skills*, http://dx.doi.org/10.1787/9789264258051-en.

StatLink http://dx.doi.org/10.1787/888933573354

References

Acemoglu, D. and D. Autor (2011), "Chapter 12 - Skills, tasks and technologies: Implications for employment and earnings", in *Handbook of Labor Economics*, Card, D. and O. Ashenfelter (eds.), 4, Part B:1043–1171, Elsevier, www.sciencedirect.com/science/article/pii/S0169721811024105.

Australian Government, Department of Education and Training (2017), Inspiring all Australians in digital literacy and STEM, www.education.gov.au/inspiring-all-australians-digital-literacy-and-stem (accessed 3 April 2017).

The Australian Industry Group (2016), *Workforce Development Needs Survey Report*. http://cdn.aigroup.com.au/Reports/2016/15396_skills_survey_report_mt_edits_2.pdf?_cldee=Z3JhaGFtLnR1cm5lckBhaWdyb3VwLmNvbS5hdQ%3d%3d&recipientid=contact-5622c0dde9fb4f51a93872c8a5920899-0019e63eeb76407394f57121ca91d9e3&esid=30016946-24c0-e611-80d0-0050568007a5.

Australian Qualifications Framework Council (2009), *Building Better Connected Learning Through Improved Student Pathways: Pathways Project Technical Report*, Pathways Project, AQFC, Adelaide, http://pandora.nla.gov.au/pan/123281/20131109-0001/www.aqf.edu.au/wp-content/uploads/2013/06/Pathways-Project-Technical-Report-November-2009.pdf

Bostock, S. and A. Steptoe (2012), "Association between low functional health literacy and mortality in older adults: Longitudinal cohort study", *BMJ*, Vol. 344, https://doi.org/10.1136/bmj.e1602.

Grotlüschen, A., et al. (2016), "Adults with low proficiency in literacy or numeracy", *OECD Education Working Papers*, No. 131, OECD Publishing, Paris, http://dx.doi.org/10.1787/5jm0v44bnmnx-en.

Kuczera M., S. Field and H. Windisch (2016), *Building Skills for All: A Review of England. Policy Insights from the Survey of Adult Skills*, www.oecd.org/edu/skills-beyond-school/building-skills-for-all-review-of-england.pdf.

Musset, P. (2015), *Building Skills for All: A Review of Finland*, www.oecd.org/education/skills-beyond-school/Building-Skills-For-All-A-Review-of-Finland.pdf.

National Innovation and Science Agenda (2017), Opportunities for women in science, technology, engineering and maths, www.innovation.gov.au/page/opportunities-women-stem (accessed 3 April 2017).

OECD (2016), *Skills Matter: Further Results from the Survey of Adult Skills*, OECD Publishing, Paris, http://dx.doi.org/10.1787/9789264258051-en.

OECD (2013a*), Time for the U.S. to Reskill?: What the Survey of Adult Skills Says*, OECD Publishing, Paris, http://dx.doi.org/10.1787/9789264204904-en.

OECD (2013b), *OECD Skills Outlook 2013: First Results from the Survey of Adult Skills*, OECD Publishing, Paris, http://dx.doi.org/10.1787/9789264204256-en.

Paccagnella, M. (2016), "Age, ageing and skills: Results from the Survey of Adult Skills", *OECD Education Working Papers*, No. 132, OECD Publishing, Paris, http://dx.doi.org/10.1787/5jm0q1n38lvc-en.

Vignoles, A., A. De Coulon and O. Marcenaro-Gutierrez (2010), "The value of basic skills in the British labour market." *Oxford Economic Papers*, July, https://doi.org/10.1093/oep/gpq012.

Chapter 2. Strengths of the skills system in Australia

> *This chapter focuses on the strengths of the Australian skills system that the country can build on. It focuses on three main findings: strong basic skills in the migrant population, widespread knowledge of ICT in Australian society, and the positive role of workplaces in skills development. The first strength is a large population of relatively skilled and well-educated migrants that bring highly desirable and much-needed skills to the workforce. Second, by international standards, adults in Australia, across all age groups, have strong computer and ICT skills, a point of key importance given concerns that automation and digitalisation might result in a jobless future for those without such skills. Finally, jobs in Australia provide more learning opportunities, including for those with low skills, than jobs in many other countries. The workplace is therefore an important and strong element of the skills system in Australia.*

The statistical data for Israel are supplied by and are under the responsibility of the relevant Israeli authorities. The use of such data by the OECD is without prejudice to the status of the Golan Heights, East Jerusalem and Israeli settlements in the West Bank under the terms of international law.

Strength 1: Immigrants in Australia are well skilled

The share of migrants in Australia

According to the Survey of Adult Skills (PIAAC), 27% of 16-65 year-olds or over four million people in Australia were born abroad. 11% are second generation immigrants (born in Australia but both parents were born abroad). Australia has, alongside New Zealand, the highest share of migrant population (foreign born) among all participating countries. Most foreign born live in New South Wales and Victoria.

What are the skills of migrants?

Strong performance of second generation migrants

In Australia, contrary to many other countries, second generation migrants have skills comparable to skills of those who were born in Australia and whose both parents were born in Australia. The integration of migrants, as measured by basic skills levels of their offspring, therefore does not seem to be a challenge in Australia (see Figure A A.1 in Annex A). For this reason, the following part of this section will only focus on two categories:

- *immigrants*: foreign born
- *natives*: native born (including second generation immigrants)

In the majority of countries, Australia included, the native population perform better than migrants. However, in Australia, the difference in performance by migration status is smaller than in many other countries (see Figure 2.1).

Figure 2.1. Share of low-skilled adults among immigrants and natives, by age

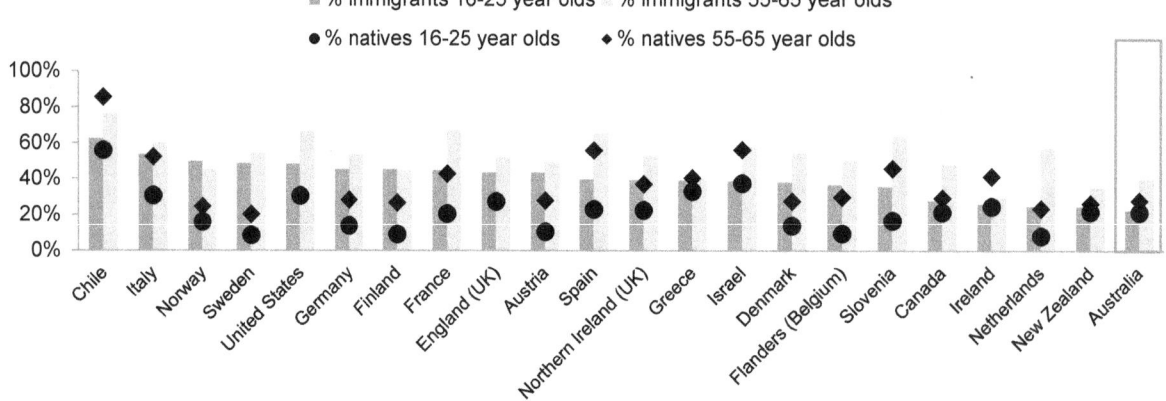

Note: The Czech Republic, Estonia, Japan, Korea, Lithuania, Poland, Slovak Republic and Turkey were excluded because there were not enough observations.
Source: OECD calculations based on OECD (2016a), *Survey of Adult Skills (PIAAC)* (Database 2012, 2015), www.oecd.org/site/piaac/publicdataandanalysis.htm.

StatLink http://dx.doi.org/10.1787/888933573373

Australia tends to attract highly skilled young people from abroad

Australia has the lowest share of young migrants with low skills among all participating countries. The difference in skills among migrant and native populations in Australia is explained by the gap in performance among older adults, as there is no gap in performance by migration status among 16-25 year-olds.

Language background influences literacy and numeracy score

Knowledge of the host country's language is critical for literacy proficiency. It is also important for numeracy as this is mediated by literacy skills in the Survey of Adult Skills. Migrants in Australia whose mother tongue is the same as the language of assessment (English) perform much better than migrants whose mother tongue is not English. This gap in performance may reflect a better mastery of the language of assessment among English mother tongue speakers, but it can also be explained by the difference among these two populations, for example, migrants with English mother tongue may have a more advantageous socio-economic background or be better educated. While around half of migrants in Australia are of English mother tongue, the remaining half need to learn English to successfully function in the host country. Poor mastery of English is a barrier to reaching full potential in literacy and numeracy skills (as assessed in English). Immigrants, who would have scored highly had they been tested in their mother tongue, may benefit particularly from learning English. This is consistent with evidence showing that improved host country language skills among migrants, particularly well-qualified individuals, leads to fast gains in literacy and numeracy (Chiswick, 1991; Dustmann and Fabbri, 2003).

The background and labour market situation of migrants

Migrants in Australia are highly educated

Migrants in Australia are better educated than migrants in other participating countries. They are also well educated in comparison to those native born. Migrants in Australia are twice as likely as native-born Australians to have a tertiary degree (bachelor degree, graduate certificate and graduate diploma, master's degree or doctoral degree). Only 12% of immigrants in Australia have below upper-secondary education, compared to 30% among natives.

Immigrants with low-educated parents are much more likely to perform poorly than those native born

Immigrants are better educated than native Australians, but they also have parents with higher levels of education. Around 40% of immigrants have at least one parent who has attained a tertiary degree, compared to 23% of native born.

The link between family background and performance in basic skills is stronger for migrants than for those native born. When neither parent has attained upper-secondary education, immigrants are almost twice as likely to be low skilled than the native population (40% comparing to 23%). Migrants with a disadvantaged socio-economic background are thus particularly at risk of developing skills shortages.

Figure 2.2. Share of adults with tertiary education, by immigrant background

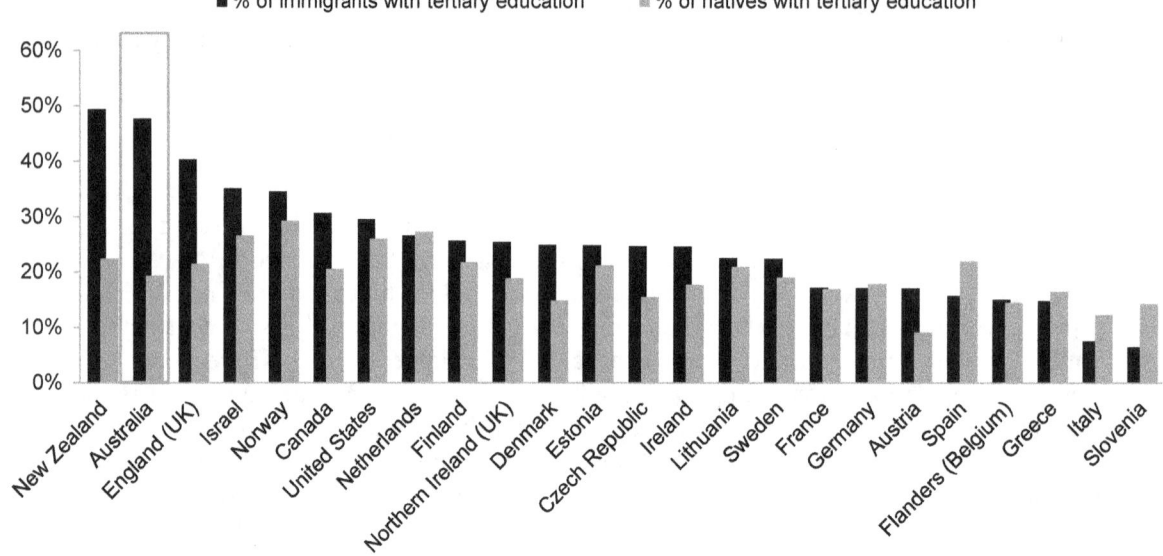

Note: Chile, Korea, Japan, Poland, the Slovak Republic and Turkey are excluded due to small sample size.
Source: OECD calculations based on OECD (2016a), *Survey of Adult Skills (PIAAC)* (Database 2012, 2015), www.oecd.org/site/piaac/publicdataandanalysis.htm.

StatLink http://dx.doi.org/10.1787/888933573392

Many migrants are working in skilled occupations

Almost 71% of migrants in Australia are employed, which is much higher than the OECD average of 66% (see Figure 2.3). Migrants in Australia are more likely to work in skilled occupations, such as legislators, senior officials and managers, professionals, technicians, and associate professionals, compared to migrants in other participating countries. Immigrants in Australia consistently earn more than immigrants in other countries. Higher levels of education and strong basic skills may largely contribute to the positive labour market outcomes of immigrants in Australia. However, when compared to natives in Australia with similar levels of education, immigrants earn less even when gender, family background and skills are taken into account.

Figure 2.3. Labour force participation by immigrant background

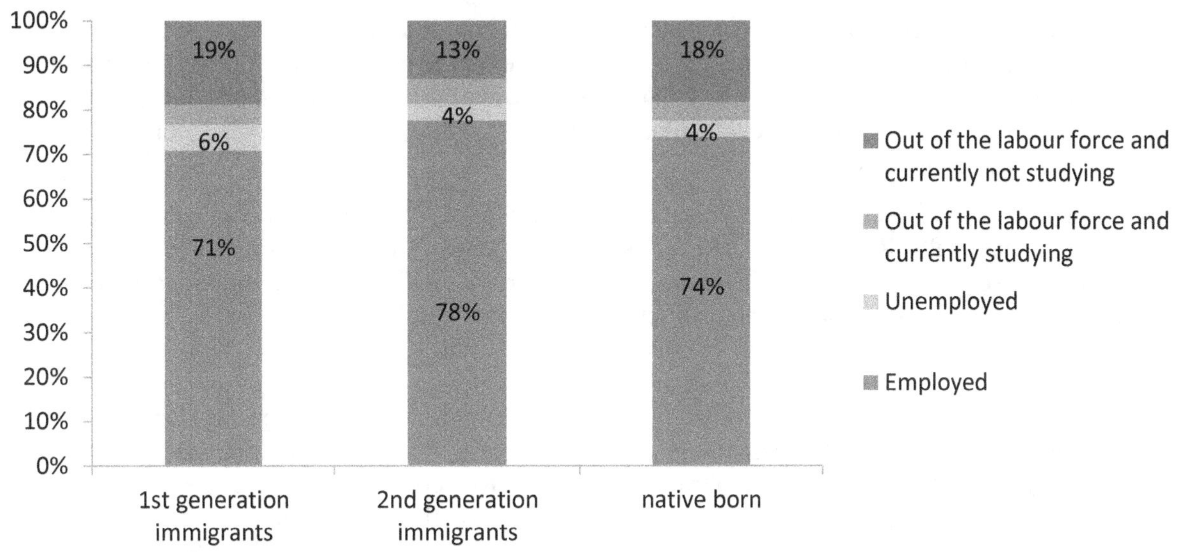

	1st generation immigrants	2nd generation immigrants	native born
Out of the labour force and currently not studying	19%	13%	18%
Out of the labour force and currently studying	6%	4%	4%
Unemployed	(included above)		
Employed	71%	78%	74%

Source: OECD calculations based on OECD (2016a), *Survey of Adult Skills (PIAAC)* (Database 2012, 2015), www.oecd.org/site/piaac/publicdataandanalysis.htm.

StatLink http://dx.doi.org/10.1787/888933573411

Conclusions

- Australia has a large population of well-skilled and well-educated migrants, many of whom are young. These skilled migrants bring highly desirable and much-needed skills to the workforce.
- Migrants in Australia are more likely to work in skilled and well-paid jobs compared to migrants in other countries. In many other countries, second-generation migrants have lower basic skills than natives. Migrants in Australia thus integrate successfully into the mainstream society, as measured by their labour market outcomes and basic skills levels of their offspring.
- Positive outcomes for migrants may be explained by the fact that migration policy in Australia gives priority to skilled migration and successfully supports newcomers in integrating into the mainstream society.
- While, on average, migrants in Australia perform very well, those with a disadvantaged socio-economic background are over-represented among low-skilled adults. Targeted policy interventions may be helpful in improving the basic skills of this group.

Strength 2: Strong performance in ICT skills

What does "Problem solving in technology-rich environments" (PSTRE) mean in the Survey of Adult Skills (PIAAC)?

Problem solving in technology-rich environments (PSTRE) is a third domain evaluated in the Survey. Proficiency in this skill reflects the capacity to use ICT devices and applications to solve the types of problems adults commonly face as ICT users in modern societies. In order to display proficiency in this domain, adults must have the basic computer skills needed to undertake an assessment on a computer: the capacity to type, manipulate a mouse, drag and drop content, and highlight text.

As with numeracy and literacy, proficiency in PSTRE is described in terms of a scale of 500 points divided into levels. In PSTRE, four levels of proficiency are defined: below Level 1, Level 1, Level 2 and Level 3. For the purpose of this study, adults scoring below Level 1 are considered as low skilled in PSTRE, while those at Level 2 or 3 are considered as highly skilled.

Out of 33 participating countries/economies in the Survey, four did not participate in the assessment of PSTRE, and in the countries that did take part, many adults opted out of the computer-based assessment. There are three main reasons for some individuals not completing the assessment on a computer and, thus, not having a score in problem solving using ICT. First, some adults had never used a computer (10% in OECD countries, 4% in Australia). Second, among the adults who had used a computer, some did not pass the ICT core test, which was designed to assess whether respondents had sufficient skill in the use of computers to complete the assessment (5% in OECD and 4% in Australia). Third, a number of respondents opted to complete the assessment in its paper-based format rather than on a computer (10% in participating countries and 14% in Australia). While those who declared no computer experience and failed the ICT score clearly lack basic computer skills, those who opted out may have done so for various reasons, such as a lack of familiarity with computers, unwillingness to use a computer for an assessment, or different field work practices across countries (OECD, 2015).

An example of a task in problem solving in technology-rich environments can be found in Annex B (Box BB.1).

Adults in Australia score high on PSTRE

Almost 40% of Australians who sat the computer assessment performed highly in PSTRE, one of the highest rates among participating countries. Australia has a very low share of adults who were not able to sit the computer assessment, but a relatively high share of adults who opted out of taking the computer-based assessment. Typically, in countries with a strong PSTRE performance the percentage of those opting out was lower than in Australia. Figure 2.4 shows the average performance of countries on PSTRE and the share of adults who did not sit the computer assessment.

Figure 2.4. Proficiency in problem solving in technology-rich environments

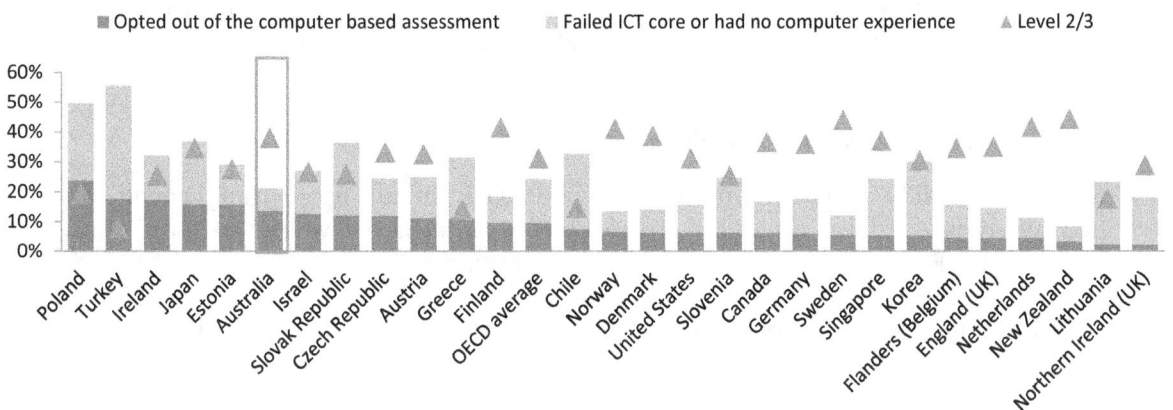

Source: OECD calculations based on OECD (2016a), *Survey of Adult Skills (PIAAC)* (Database 2012, 2015), www.oecd.org/site/piaac/publicdataandanalysis.htm.

StatLink http://dx.doi.org/10.1787/888933573430

High performance in PSTRE for all age groups

In Australia, both young (16-25 year-old) and older (55-65 year-old) adults perform better in PSTRE than their peers in corresponding age groups in many other participating countries (see Figure 2.5).

Figure 2.5. Share of adults scoring at Level 2 or 3 in PSTRE, by age group

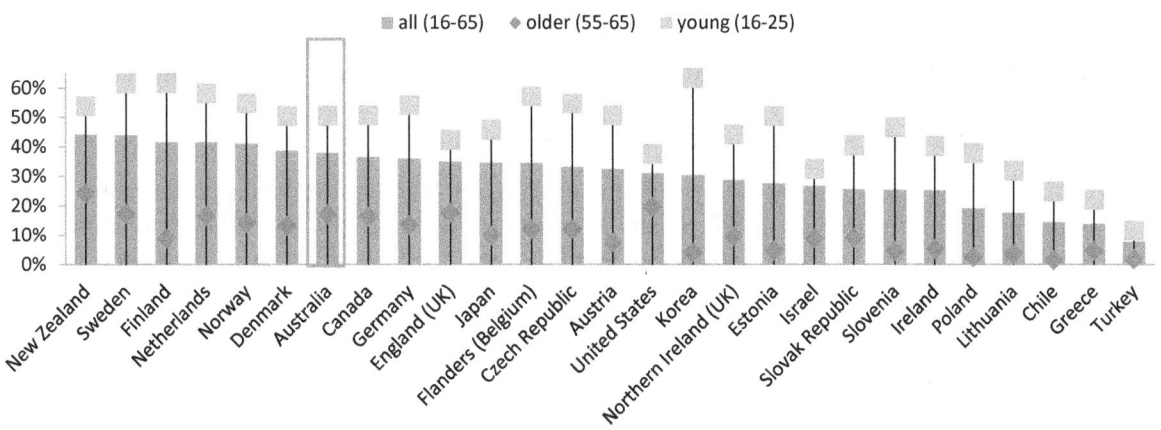

Source: OECD calculations based on OECD (2016a), *Survey of Adult Skills (PIAAC)* (Database 2012, 2015), www.oecd.org/site/piaac/publicdataandanalysis.htm.

StatLink http://dx.doi.org/10.1787/888933573449

However, performance in PSTRE is lower in older cohorts

In many countries, including Australia, young people are more familiar with ICT technologies and perform better in PSTRE than older adults: in Australia while more than half of 16-25 year-olds have strong PSTRE skills, fewer than 20% of 55-65 year-olds reach this level of proficiency. Use of ICT is widespread in Australia, with around 85% of those aged 15 and older using the Internet (The World Bank, 2016). The high penetration of ICT technology means that knowledge of ICT and computers may be required at work and to participate in political and social life. Adults lacking computer knowledge and skills therefore are more at risk of being excluded or disadvantaged in various aspects of life.

There is no difference in the performances between men and women

Gender is weakly related to proficiency in PSTRE in all participating countries, particularly in Australia, where the difference between men and woman performing at high levels in PSTRE is the smallest across OECD countries.

Australian migrants perform particularly well in PSTRE, although not as good as those native born

Immigrant and language background is correlated with the probability of performing at Level 2 or 3 in PSTRE. While, on average, migrants perform worse than those native born in Australia, the gap in performance by migration status is smaller than in other countries.

More educated adults are much more likely to have better PSTRE skills

Educational attainment and ICT use are strongly associated with PSTRE proficiency. An adult in Australia with tertiary education is 36 percentage points more likely than an adult with less than upper-secondary education to perform at Level 2 or 3 in PSTRE. Even after accounting for other factors, such as age, gender, parents' education, immigrant background, literacy proficiencies and use of ICT skills, this association remains significant. (OECD, 2015: 47). Individuals may develop higher-level PSTRE skills through education and training, and these skills may be further reinforced through work and out-of-work practices. The impact of work on PSTRE skills is mediated by education, if high levels of education and training lead to jobs involving more work with computers.

Strong PSTRE skills are associated with better labour market outcomes

Consistent with findings on literacy and numeracy skills and labour market performance, higher levels of proficiency in PSTRE are associated with better labour market outcomes. On average across OECD countries, hourly wages for workers who perform at proficiency Level 2 or 3 are 26% higher than mean hourly wages for workers who perform below Level 1 (see also Falck et al., 2016). While strong PSTRE skills in Australia also yield higher wages, the premium is lower than in most participating countries. Proficiency in PSTRE, as well as use of ICT (as measured by the use of e-mails at work), are associated with higher rates of labour force participation, even after accounting for other factors. Having a job is also linked to stronger performance. In Australia, 42% of workers have high PSTRE skills, compared to 25% of non-workers. However, it is not clear whether employment is conditional for strong PSTRE skills, or whether these skills improve through work, or both.

Conclusions

- By international standards, adults in Australia, across all age groups, have strong PSTRE skills. This is important as ICT technologies and the use of computers have changed working methods and work organisation. As a consequence,

employment in jobs subject to automation has been shrinking, along with the demand for the skills necessary to perform these jobs. This trend may accelerate in the future as technology is increasingly applied in workplaces and computers are able to perform more and more complex tasks. Adult not familiar with computers will therefore be poorly equipped to respond to new work requirements triggered by new technology.
- Policies targeting specific populations can build on good ICT knowledge among adults in Australia. They can involve, for example, career guidance provision and online learning for disadvantaged youth.

Strength 3: In Australia, the workplace is conducive to learning

Learning on-the-job encompasses a wide range of activities. Drawing on data from the Survey for Adult Skills this report distinguishes three types of on-the-job learning:

- structured on-the-job training
- learning while working
- use of skills on the job

These forms of learning often depend on the work organisation and managerial culture that influences how people interact and approach problems to be solved at work. The three types of learning are discussed separately below.

Structured on the-job training

Around 20% of low-skilled employees participate in structured training

In Australia, around one in five low-skilled adults receive on-the-job training (see Box 2.1 for the definition), which is close to the average of participating countries. However, on-the-job training encompasses various activities, and it is unclear how much of this training contributes to basic skills development. For example, narrowly defined job-specific training, such as mandatory training related to health and safety, makes a limited contribution to a person's basic skills. Without disentangling various forms of training it is therefore difficult to say how much it helps low-skilled individuals to upgrade their skills.

Box 2.1. Organised on-the-job training attended in the last 12 months

Organised on-the-job training is characterised by planned periods of training, instruction or practical experience that use the normal tools of work.

It is usually organised by the employer to facilitate the adaptation of (new) staff.

It may include general training about the company and specific job-related instructions (health and safety hazards, working practices).

It includes, for instance, organised training or instructions by management, supervisors or co-workers to help the respondent do his/her job better or to introduce him/her to new tasks. It can also take place in the presence of a tutor.

Source: OECD (2013), *Skills Outlook 2013: First Results from the Survey of Adult Skills*, Variable B_Q12c, learning while working, http://dx.doi.org/10.1787/9789264204256-en.

In Australia, the work environment favours learning while working, also among the low skilled

The Survey of Adult Skills provides information on some aspects of work that may promote learning and skills development, such as learning-by-doing from the performed tasks and learning new work-related skills from co-workers and supervisors.

In many countries, including Australia, employees with low skills are over-represented in jobs where they receive no help from co-workers and supervisors, and in jobs involving no learning while doing (presumably often jobs requiring few skills). However, by international standards, low-skilled workers in Australia have more opportunities to learn from others and by doing than in other countries. For example, in Australia, around 46% of low-skilled employees report learning-by-doing on a daily basis, one of the highest rates among OECD countries. Figure 2.6 shows how often low-skilled adults learn from others across participating countries.

Some companies are better than others at providing opportunities for learning while working

Detailed analysis shows that opportunities for learning while working, including for low-skilled adults, depend on firm characteristics. An analysis of various factors, including firm and individual characteristics, confirms that adults with stronger basic skills and higher education learn more often from others at work. It also shows that in Australia, learning from co-workers and colleagues is more common in large companies and in companies that have recently been employing. Age is negatively associated with learning from colleagues. This shows that younger workers, who presumably have less work experience, receive more advice from co-workers. It may also be that younger workers are more open to guidance from others. Adults in elementary low-skilled jobs are less exposed to relevant learning while working. When other characteristics are taken into account, gender is not associated with learning while working opportunities.

Use of skills on the job

Australian adults use their skills intensely in the workplace

The Survey of Adult Skills provides detailed information on how often respondents perform specific tasks in their jobs, such as reading, writing, numeracy, ICT skills and problem solving (OECD, 2013a). Table 2.1 describe these skills in more detail and shows how Australia compares to participating countries in terms of skills use at work among high and low-skilled workers. In many areas of skills use, such as reading, numeracy and problem solving, Australia, similar to New Zealand, ranks near the top of the distribution.

Figure 2.6. How often low-skilled workers learn work-related skills from co-workers and supervisors

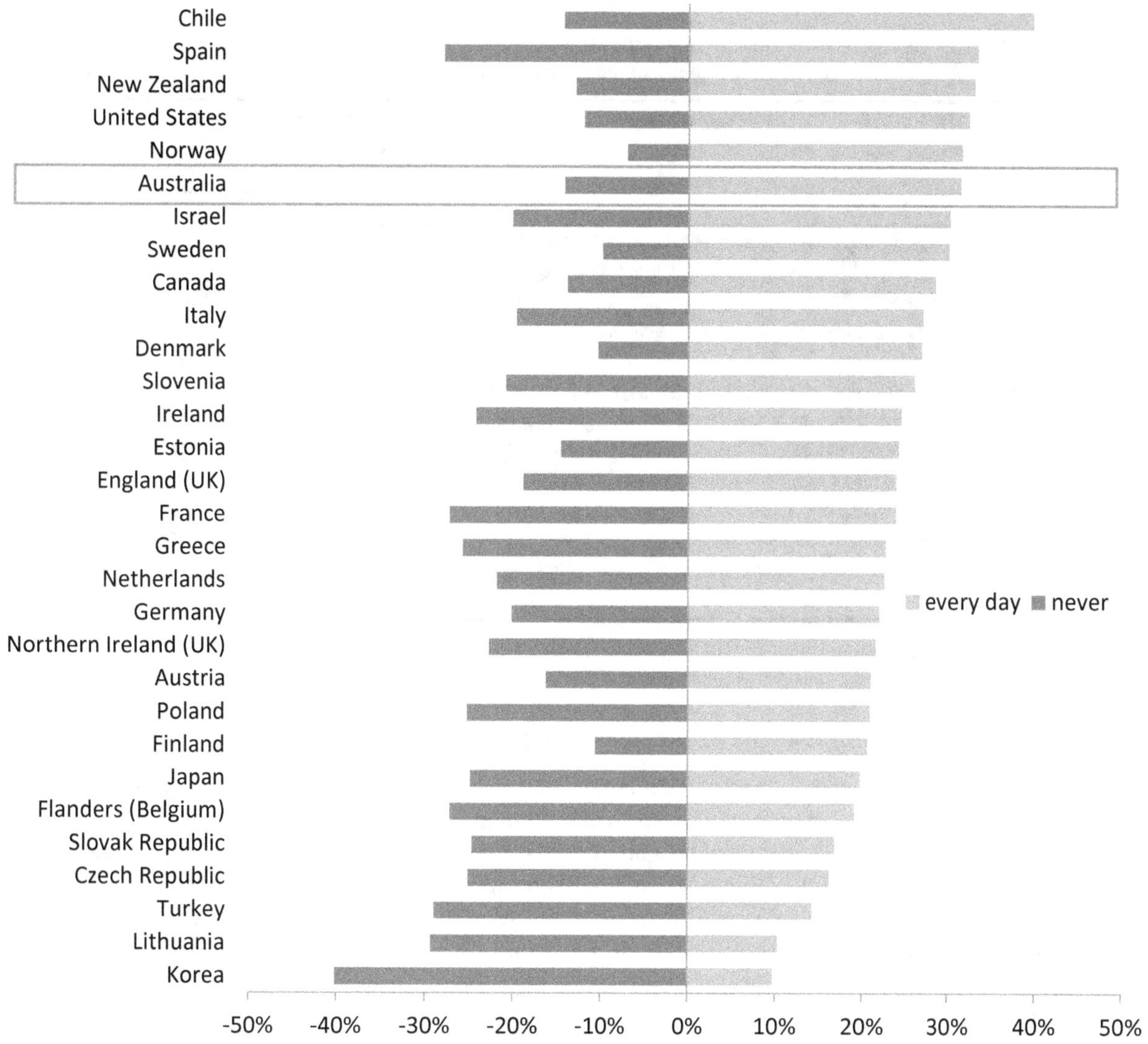

Note: The left hand (negative) side stands for the percentage of low-skilled workers who report to never learn from others. Bars on the right hand side show the percentage of low-skilled workers reporting learning every day from colleagues.
Source: OECD calculations based on OECD (2016a), *Survey of Adult Skills (PIAAC)* (Database 2012, 2015), www.oecd.org/site/piaac/publicdataandanalysis.htm.

StatLink http://dx.doi.org/10.1787/888933573468

In Australia, many low-skilled adults use basic skills at work

In Australia, those with low skills are more likely than in most countries to use reading, numeracy and problem-solving skills at work. This is positive if using these skills at work promotes the development of initially low-skilled employees. However, Survey of Adult Skills data do not allow for estimating the impact of daily work on basic skills development. It is therefore not clear whether and how many low-skilled workers improve their basic skills as a result of carrying out tasks involving basic skills on the job. On the negative side, the allocation of low-skilled individuals to tasks requiring a higher level of skills can be a sign of misallocation of human resources, especially if tasks performed on the job have no or low effect on the basic skills of the employee.

Table 2.1. Low skilled in Australia use their skills in the workplace more often than their peers in other countries

Use of specific skills by low-and highly skilled (literacy and/or numeracy) workers in Australia in comparison with use of the same skills in other countries

	The tasks involved	Use of these skills in Australia in comparison to the average of participating countries	
		Low skilled	Highly skilled
Reading	Reading documents (directions, instructions, letters, memos, e-mails, articles, books, manuals, bills, invoices, diagrams, maps).	5th ranking	2nd ranking
Writing	Writing documents (letters, memos, e-mails, articles, reports, forms).	10th ranking	6th ranking
Numeracy	Calculating prices, costs or budgets; use of fractions, decimals or percentages; use of calculators; preparing graphs or tables; algebra or formulas.	5th ranking	3rd ranking
ICT skills	Using e-mail, Internet, spreadsheets, word processors, programming languages; conducting transactions on line; participating in online discussions.	15th ranking	8th ranking
Problem solving	Facing complex problems (at least 30 minutes of thinking to find a solution).	3rd ranking	3rd ranking

Source: OECD calculations based on OECD (2016), *Survey of Adult Skills (PIAAC)* (Database 2012, 2015), www.oecd.org/site/piaac/publicdataandanalysis.htm.

There are gender differences in the use of some skills at work

In Australia, as in many other participating countries, men use numeracy and problem solving at work more often than women; while women are as likely as men to use reading and writing skills. There is no gender gap in ICT skills in Australia. Differences in the use at work of numeracy and problem-solving skills between men and women may reflect the self-selection of women into specific sectors and jobs that rely less on numeracy skills. Gender differences in the use of skills start early on in life, and already in school children are sorted into different fields of study, with boys being more likely to choose fields requiring stronger numeracy skills than girls. If work contributes to the development of skills, the over-representation of women in jobs where numeracy and problem solving are less commonly used can further reinforce the gender gap in skills. The issue of gender preferences and its impact on skills will be further explored in Chapter 3.

Conclusions

- People develop their skills in the workplace. They learn at work through more formalised training, but also by daily interactions with colleagues and supervisors, and simply by doing the work. Jobs in Australia provide more learning opportunities, including for those with low skills, than jobs in many other countries. The workplace is therefore an important and strong element of the skills system in Australia.
- Drawing on this positive experience, Australia could promote and scale up work arrangements and management practices that lead to the best outcomes in terms of skills improvement.

References

Chiswick, B. R. (1991), "Speaking, reading, and earnings among low-skilled immigrants." *Journal of Labor Economics,* Vol. 9/2, pp. 149-70.

Dustmann, C. and F. Fabbri (2003), "Language proficiency and labour market performance of immigrants in the UK.", *The Economic Journal,* Vol. 113/ 489, pp. 695–717, http://dx.doi.org/10.1111/1468-0297.t01-1-00151.

Falck, O., A. Heimisch and S. Wiederhold (2016), "Returns to ICT skills", *OECD Education Working Papers*, No. 134, OECD Publishing, Paris, http://dx.doi.org/10.1787/5jlzfl2p5rzq-en.

OECD (2015), *Adults, Computers and Problem Solving: What's the Problem?,* OECD Publishing, Paris, http://dx.doi.org/10.1787/9789264236844-en.

OECD (2013), *Skills Outlook 2013: First Results from the Survey of Adult Skills*, OECD Publishing, Paris, http://dx.doi.org/10.1787/9789264204256-en.

The World Bank (2016), Internet users (per 100 people), http://data.un.org/Data.aspx?d=WDI&f=Indicator_Code%3AIT.NET.USER.P2#WDI, (accessed 17 December 2016).

Chapter 3. Numeracy skills are not as good as literacy skills in Australia

Australians have among the best literacy skills compared with other countries participating in the Survey of Adult Skills (PIAAC). At the same time, their performance in numeracy is only average and there is evidence suggesting that numeracy skills have been declining in recent years. Mathematics performances among students in secondary education could usefully be improved. But this chapter also points to a significant gender difference in numeracy performance, with women scoring lower than men and being underrepresented in science, technology, engineering and mathematics (STEM) occupations. Policies to attract and retain more women in the STEM workforce would help to reduce occupational segmentation in the labour force and improve gender equity in labour market outcomes.

The statistical data for Israel are supplied by and are under the responsibility of the relevant Israeli authorities. The use of such data by the OECD is without prejudice to the status of the Golan Heights, East Jerusalem and Israeli settlements in the West Bank under the terms of international law.

Characteristics of adults with low numeracy skills

Around three million Australians have low numeracy skills

Australians have among the best literacy skills across countries participating in the Survey of Adult Skills, a product of the OECD Programme for the International Assessment of Adult Competencies (PIAAC), however, their performance in numeracy is average (see Figure 3.1). One Australian in five performs below Level 2 in numeracy, which means that around three million Australians struggle with the numerical reasoning necessary to cope with everyday situations (such as reading a petrol gauge). While many other countries are doing better in literacy than in numeracy, the difference between literacy and numeracy scores is not nearly as significant as in Australia. In Australia, 13% of adults with higher literacy skills (Level 2 and above in the Survey) perform poorly in numeracy, compared to 10% among participating countries. Underperformance in numeracy is observed in Australia across all age groups, including young people (16-24 year-olds), and across all levels of educational attainment. For example, 7% of all tertiary graduates have low numeracy skills compared to 3% with low literacy skills.

Inequality in distribution of numeracy performance

Australia, in comparison with other countries, has considerable inequalities in the distribution of numeracy scores, which signals large gaps between the lowest and the best performers. In Australia, 182 score points separate the highest and the lowest 5% of performers in numeracy, far above the participating country average of 167 score points. Only the United States has a wider gap between the lowest and the highest performers.

Significant gender difference in numeracy performances

While men and women in Australia have similar literacy skills, men perform better in numeracy. The gender gap in Australia is, on average, slightly more significant than in participating countries. The gender gap among young adults is narrower than among older adults. This may be because the school system is now more effective in conveying numeracy skills to girls than in the past, or because an initially narrow gender gap in numeracy widens later in life due to the lower participation of women in the labour market and the over-representation of women in jobs requiring lower numeracy skills and in part-time employment.

Women are less likely to enter science, technology, engineering and mathematics (STEM) fields

Evidence shows that girls and boys tend to absorb, and act on, gender stereotypes about school subjects early on in their schooling (OECD, 2011; 2013). These stereotypes may influence young people's choices of fields of study. This determines the skills they develop, as some fields of study may require stronger numeracy skills than others. In Australia, as in many other countries, boys are far more likely than girls to choose mathematics and science (Kennedy et al., 2014). Women in Australia studying at post-secondary and tertiary levels are less likely to graduate in science (40% of graduates), and much less likely to graduate in fields of study such as engineering, manufacturing and construction (25% of graduates) (OECD, 2016, Table A3.3).

Figure 3.1. Literacy and numeracy skills, by levels

16-65 year-olds (2012, 2015)

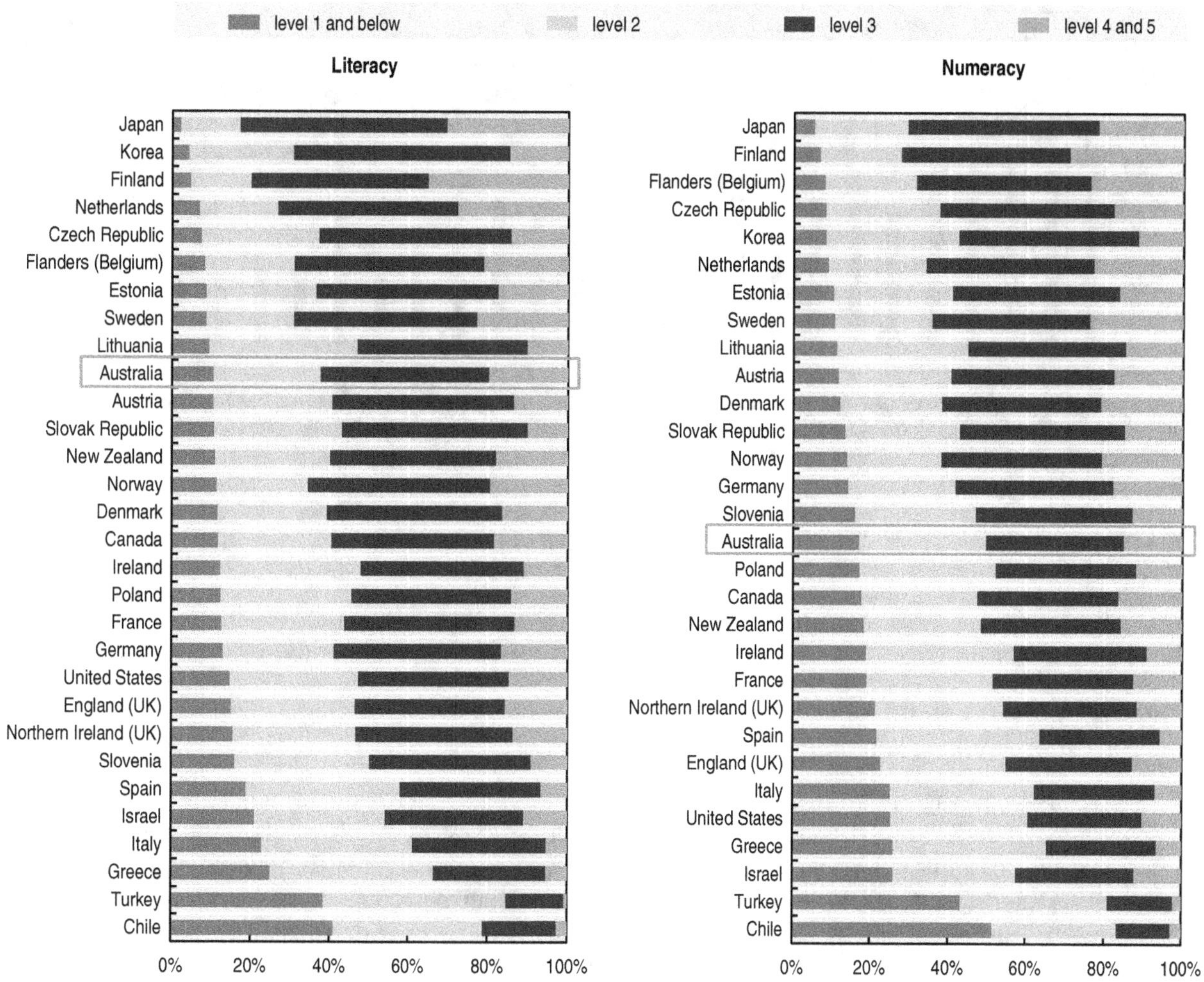

■ level 1 and below ■ level 2 ■ level 3 ■ level 4 and 5

Note: Adults who obtained their highest qualification outside the host country, those with foreign qualifications and first-generation migrants who obtained their highest qualification prior to entering the host country, are excluded.
Source: OECD calculations based on OECD (2016a), *Survey of Adult Skills (PIAAC)* (Database 2012, 2015), www.oecd.org/site/piaac/publicdataandanalysis.htm.

StatLink ⟶ http://dx.doi.org/10.1787/888933573487

Immigrants also score lower on numeracy than literacy

In Australia, the skill gap between natives (born in Australia) and immigrants (foreign born), including in numeracy, is smaller than in most participating countries. However, the gap between literacy and numeracy scores among immigrants remains as significant as in the native population (12 point difference).

Figure 3.2. Performance of immigrants in numeracy and literacy

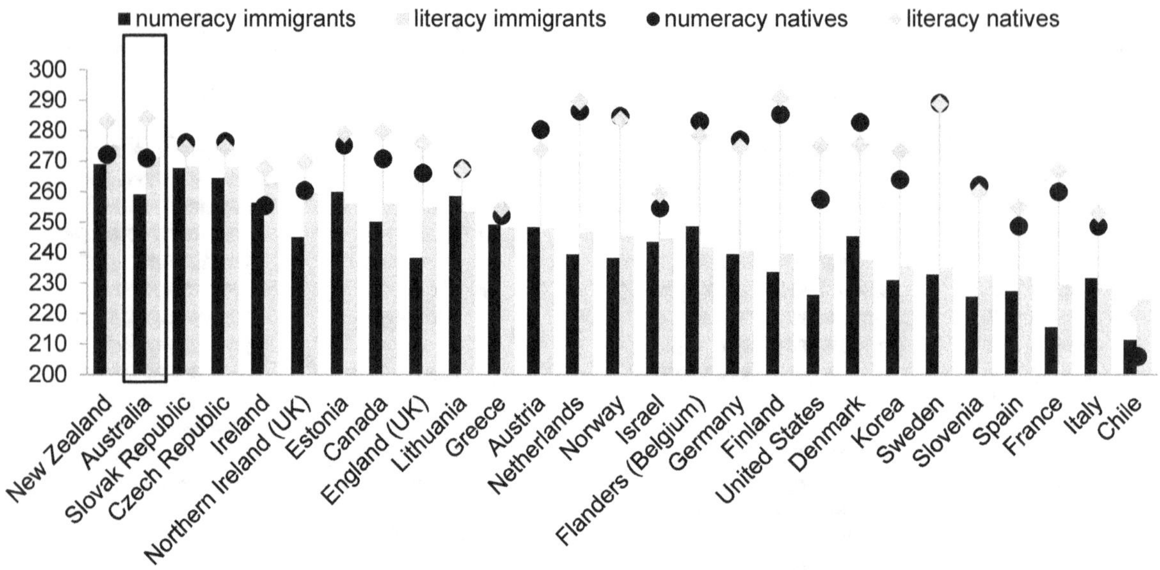

Note: Japan, Poland and Turkey are excluded due to small sample size.
Source: OECD calculations based on OECD (2016a), *Survey of Adult Skills (PIAAC)* (Database 2012, 2015), www.oecd.org/site/piaac/publicdataandanalysis.htm.

StatLink http://dx.doi.org/10.1787/888933573506

Declining numeracy skills

Trends in average performances in numeracy (and literacy) provide an indicator of how school systems are evolving over the years. The Survey of Adult Skills only gives a snapshot of adult performance in 2012; however, in combination with other comparable OECD surveys it can be used to track how Australian performance has evolved over recent years. The Survey of Adult Skills was designed to provide reliable comparisons with the results of the International Adult Literacy Survey (IALS), which was administered between 1994 and 1998, and the Adult Literacy and Life Skills Survey (ALL), administered between 2003 and 2007. Australia participated in all three surveys. The average literacy scores of adults in Australia slightly increased during this period, from 272 in IALS to 277 in ALL and finally 280 in PIAAC. A numeracy test was introduced in ALL, and the numeracy score declined from 272 in ALL to 268 in PIAAC (Paccagnella, 2016). These results indicate that adults nowadays may have lower numeracy skills than adults 10 years ago.

Trends in mathematics

The OECD Programme for International Student Assessment (PISA) evaluates education systems worldwide by periodically testing the skills and knowledge of 15-year-old students. PISA reviews the extent to which students near the end of compulsory education have acquired some of the knowledge and skills essential for their full participation in modern society, particularly in mathematics, reading and science. Although the PISA mathematic scores of young Australians are above average, the results show that over the years, the numeracy skills of 15-year-olds may have declined. From 2003, the mean mathematics score of 15-year-old Australians continuously decreased (in PISA 2003,

2006, 2009 and 2012 results). Of the 64 countries with PISA trend data, 25 show an average annual improvement in mathematics performances between 2003 and 2012, 25 show no change, and 14 (Australia included) show an average deterioration in performance. Most countries with a similar performance to Australia in 2003 (such as Belgium (Flanders), Japan or Switzerland) improved their results over the years, while in the Czech Republic and New Zealand results worsened between 2003 and 2012. Australian reading scores in PISA have also declined over the years, although the rate of deceleration was smaller than for mathematics. The change in PISA scores could be explained by the difference in cohorts taking the test (15-year-olds assessed in 2003 are different to 15-year-olds taking the test in 2012). Declining results may also be due to a worsening performance of the school system.

Above-average PISA mathematics scores at the age of 15 transform to below average performances at the age of 20-22 in PIAAC

PISA and PIAAC results could, to a certain extent, be compared to track the development of skills in young adults. However, the results need to be treated with caution as the conclusions draw on a comparison of two independent cross-sectional datasets administered at different points of time. Students aged 15 who participated in PISA 2000 reappear as 27-year-olds in PIAAC, similarly those who participated in PISA 2003 are aged 24 in PIAAC 2012. The PISA/PIAAC comparison shows that 15-year-old Australian students have above-average numeracy scores in all PISA cycles from 2000 to 2012, but a below-average performance among the relevant age cohorts in PIAAC. For example 15-year-olds in 2006 perform above average in numeracy in PISA, but by the age of 20-22 their numeracy skills fall below the average in the Survey of Adult Skills (PIAAC). Strengths in numeracy skills among 15-year-old Australians transform to weaknesses in basic numeracy skills as young adults. Other top performers in numeracy in PISA, such as Japan, Finland or the Netherlands, maintain their top position in the Survey of Adult Skills (PIAAC). The drop of Australia in the country ranking between PISA and the Survey of Adult Skills only applies to numeracy proficiencies. In literacy, Australia is among the best performing countries in both assessments. Development of numeracy skills therefore represents a key challenge in Australia.

Figure 3.3. Performance of young people in PISA and in PIAAC

Comparison of 15-year-olds in PISA assessment with 20-22 year-olds in PIAAC assessment

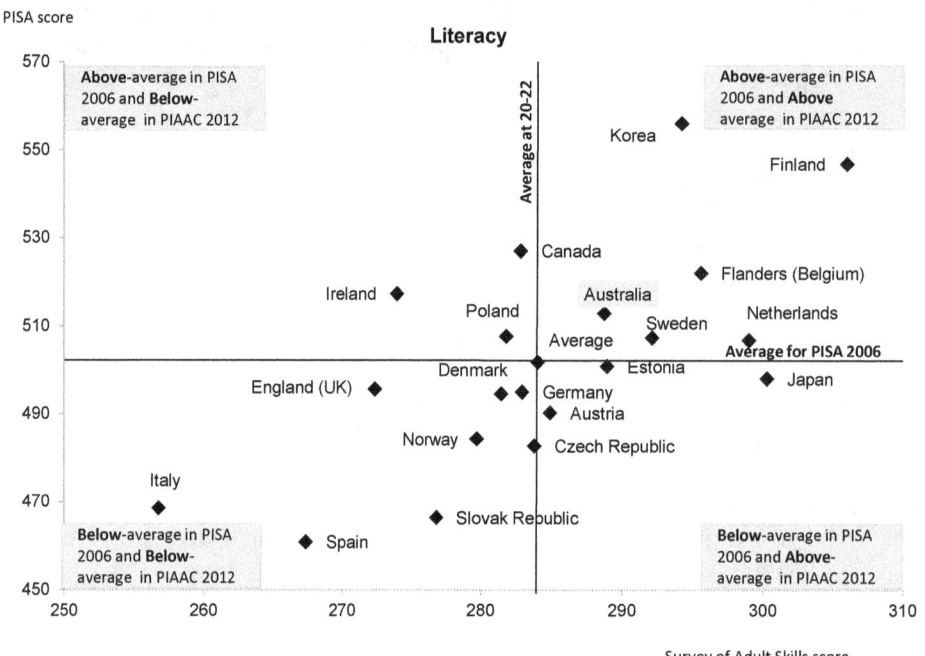

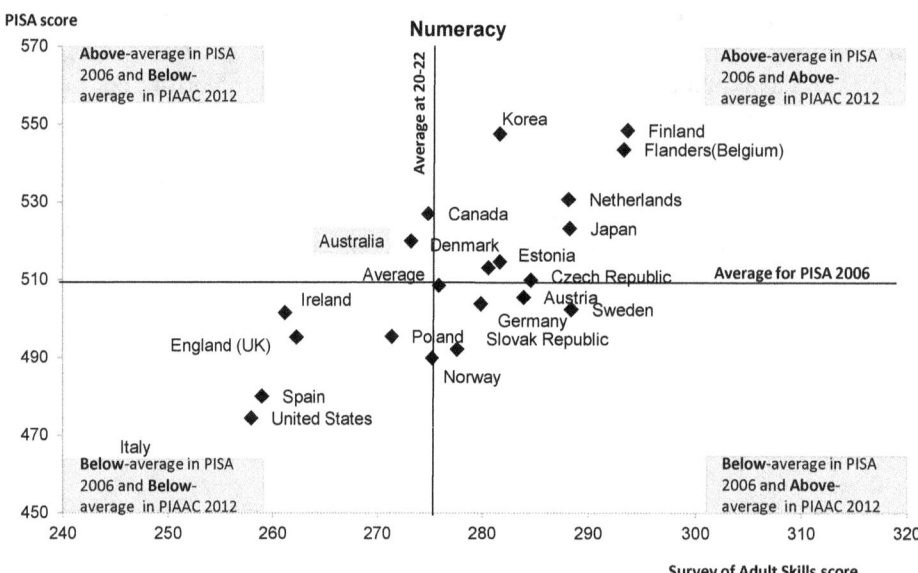

Note: How to read this chart: These charts show how 15-year-old students performed in PISA relative to other countries, and how the same cohorts scored, again relative to other countries, as young adults a few years later in the Survey of Adult Skills. For example, the 15-year-olds in the United States had below-average numeracy scores in 2006. Six years later, 21-year-old US adults also had below-average scores in the Survey of Adult Skills. Countries in the top right quadrant (e.g. Korea, Finland) had above-average scores on both assessments.

The average presented here is a refinement of the average presented in the main report of the Survey of Adult Skills (OECD, 2013a). It refers to the arithmetic mean of country estimates, restricted to the set of countries that participated in both the Survey of Adult Skills and the corresponding round of PISA.

Source: OECD (2012), *Survey of Adult Skills (PIAAC),* Database 2012, www.oecd.org/site/piaac/publicdataandanalysis.htm; OECD (2006), PISA database 2006, www.oecd.org/pisa/pisaproducts/database-pisa2006.htm.

StatLink http://dx.doi.org/10.1787/888933573525

The consequences of not having good numeracy skills

Numeracy skills assessed by the Survey of Adult Skills (PIAAC) refer to mathematical reasoning required to manage and solve real life problems. Numeracy skills are not about abstract mathematics, but about applying mathematical concepts to daily situations in all aspects of life. For example, some people with low basic numeracy skills (Level 2 or below) may not be able to read a petrol gauge to estimate how much petrol is left in the car's fuel tank. From a policy point of view it is therefore reasonable to expect all citizens to acquire at least basic numeracy skills.

Better numeracy skills are associated with higher earnings and higher employment rates

Both higher numeracy and literacy are associated with stronger labour market performance and social outcomes, even when other factors, such as years of education, age, gender, spoken language, and parental education and years of education are taken into account. In Australia, an increase of 50 points on the numeracy scale (corresponding to a difference between two levels of proficiency) is associated with a 10% increase in wages for men and 6% for women.

Using 2012 PIAAC data, Lane and Conlon (2016) showed that there are significantly higher earnings and employment returns to increasing levels of formally recognised education and to increasing levels of numeracy and literacy skills proficiencies, when controlling for the level of education. In particular, they found that in the majority of OECD countries, numeracy skills are associated with higher earnings compared to equivalent literacy levels (at each level of education). Compared to literacy skills, the authors demonstrated that numeracy skills have a much more significant impact on employment outcomes.

Strong numeracy skills will be required in the labour market

"The Australian Government estimates that up to 75% of areas with the fastest-growing jobs will require science, technology, engineering or mathematics skills" (Cook, 2015). Filling these jobs could represent a challenge given shortages in numeracy skills among many adults, including young people, in Australia. Already, 25% of employers report having difficulties with recruiting workers with STEM skills (The Australian Industry Group, 2016). As a result, Australia may lose out in the technological race against countries with a large pool of well-skilled individuals.

Recommendations: How to tackle low performance in numeracy

Policy pointer 1: Increase participation of women in STEM fields

Breakdown stereotypes to encourage women to enter STEM fields

Gender differences in educational choices are often related to student attitudes (motivation, interest) in studying a particular subject, rather than their ability and school performance. Young women often do not translate their good school performance into choosing a field of study that offers better employment prospects, such as studies in STEM fields. If policy were able to attract and retain more women in the STEM workforce, this would increase the number of scientists and engineers overall, thus promoting research, innovation and, ultimately, long term growth. Such policies would also help reduce occupational segmentation in the labour force and improve gender equity in labour market outcomes overall (Finnie and Frenette, 2003; AAUW, 2015).

The Australian Government recently introduced initiatives to increase participation in STEM fields

The Australian Government's National Innovation and Science Agenda, announced in December 2015, provides AUS 112 million over four years from 2016-17 for initiatives increasing the participation of all students in STEM and improving their digital literacy. These initiatives target school-age students and those in the early learning years. They encourage more women to choose and stay in STEM research and related careers. The government is also providing AUS 28 million over four years for 1 400 new industry internships for PhD researchers with a focus on supporting women to choose to study and work in STEM.

Example of successful initiatives: How other countries overcome job stereotypes in schools

The under-representation of women in STEM fields is common in many countries. In response to this challenge, various initiatives have been developed. Box 3.1 describes Inspiring the Future, a United Kingdom initiative by Education and Employers that aims to break down job gender stereotypes at school in the United Kingdom.

Box 3.1. Inspiring the Future: Career guidance and gender

This initiative aims to raise aspirations by helping young people understand the link between learning in school and the world of work in order to motivate them to improve their academic performance. One of the aims of Inspiring the Future is to break down job gender stereotypes among young people and encourage girls and boys to envisage jobs that are traditionally associated with the other gender (watch the video presenting the Inspiring the Future initiative www.youtube.com/watch?v=qv8VZVP5csA).

Inspiring the Future connects primary and secondary schools and volunteers from the world of work. Volunteers represent different sectors and positions and range from apprentices to chief executives. They talk informally to young people about their job and career route in schools near where they live or work. Teachers and volunteers are connected through a secure website. Teachers select and invite people who best meet the needs of their students from a range of sectors and professions.

Source: Education and Employers Taskforce (2016), *Inspiring the Future*, www.educationandemployers.org/programmes/inspiring-the-future/.

Policy pointer 2: Strengthen the focus on mathematics throughout secondary education

Poor numeracy performance of young upper-secondary graduates in Australia

International comparison shows that while young adults in Australia have strong literacy skills, in numeracy they lag behind their peers with comparable qualifications, for both academic and vocational education and training (VET) orientation (see Table 3.1. Basic skills demands of upper-secondary qualifications across countries). While this finding cannot directly be connected to the design of the school system in Australia, it raises questions about the effectiveness of the school system in developing strong numeracy skills in young people.

Table 3.1. Basic skills demands of upper-secondary qualifications across countries

A comparison of numeracy and literacy skills of 16-34 year-olds with upper-secondary qualifications across countries, with qualifications broken down into academic and vocational

	Numeracy		Literacy	
	Academic	VET	Academic	VET
Australia	279 (3)	266 (3)	294 (3)	274 (3)
Austria	311 (4)	274 (2)	307 (3)	272 (2)
Denmark	299 (3)	278 (3)	300 (2)	269 (3)
Finland	311 (2)	280 (2)	319 (2)	290 (2)
France	285 (2)	248 (2)	295 (2)	260 (2)
Germany	306 (3)	268 (3)	308 (2)	267 (3)
Norway	293 (3)	276 (3)	319 (2)	286 (2)
Netherlands	314 (2)	279 (2)	294 (2)	275 (3)
Spain	270 (2)	254 (7)	278 (2)	258 (5)

Note: Standard errors in brackets.
Source: OECD calculations based on OECD (2016a), *Survey of Adult Skills (PIAAC)* (Database 2012, 2015), www.oecd.org/site/piaac/publicdataandanalysis.htm.

The share of upper-secondary students studying science and advanced mathematics has declined

In Australia, education is compulsory until the age of 16, which roughly corresponds to the end of lower-secondary school (Australian Government, 2016). Beyond this point, students can chose senior secondary education (years 11 and 12) that ends with a senior secondary certificate providing access to higher education institutions. They can also follow a vocational education and training route. In Australia, while English is compulsory throughout senior secondary school in nearly the whole country, mathematics is compulsory only in some parts of Australia (Kennedy et al., 2014). Many students can therefore choose not to study mathematics in the second stage of their secondary education. Kennedy et al., (2014) show that between 1992 and 2012, the percentage of students studying advanced and intermediate mathematics and science declined. According to some studies, the diversification of subjects students can choose from was the most likely cause of the decline (Phillips, 2016).

The Australian Government has launched initiatives to improve mathematics performances among young people

The Australian Government has launched many initiatives to address the challenge of low numeracy skills among young people. It has provided AUS 7.4 million (through the Inquiry project) to improve the teaching practices, student engagement and learning outcomes in mathematics. Free online resources developed by the Australian Academy of Science will support this project. They will help students to deal with complex situations using a variety of mathematical methods drawing on real-world examples. The classroom resources for Foundation to Year 10 will have a particular focus on understanding, reasoning and problem solving. In addition, a range of professional learning resources will promote individual teacher learning and whole-school change.

Example of successful initiatives: How other countries tackle low numeracy skills

England (United Kingdom) is one of the countries where, until recently, students could opt out of mathematics and English before the age of 16. For example, 16-year-old students passing the final secondary exam (GCSE) could choose not to pass it in mathematics and English. National evaluations, such as Skills for Life Surveys, and international studies, such as the International Survey of Adult Skills, pointed out that the system was failing in developing strong basic skills for young people. In response, a range of reforms reinforcing the position of English and mathematics in the education system was introduced, described in Box 3.2.

Box 3.2. Reform of the school system in England (United Kingdom)

More young people are now required to continue with English and mathematics

To increase completion rates and improve basic skills among young people, the age of compulsory education has been raised from 16 to 18. English and mathematics have become mandatory for all students passing their GCSEs (a secondary exam typically taken by 16-year-olds). Since August 2014, students aged between 16 and 19 who have not achieved a good pass in English and/or mathematics at GCSE by age 16 must continue to work towards achieving either these qualifications or an approved interim qualification. The new requirements apply to all young people, including those in apprenticeships and vocational programmes.

New initiatives seek the better preparation of further education teachers of mathematics and English

With a view to upskilling the workforce in upper-secondary institutions (mainly further colleges) in the teaching of mathematics and English, a GBP 30 million package was put in place for 2014/2015. It includes bursaries of GBP 9 000 for English teachers, and of GBP 20 000 for mathematics teachers to attract good graduates into teaching. There are also programmes to enhance the skills of existing mathematics and English teachers so that they can teach at GCSE level. Support has also been offered for professional development for up to 2 000 teachers who want to teach mathematics to GCSE level. The new Education and Training Foundation (ETF) is seeking to improve standards in teaching and learning including English and mathematics. The Office for Standards in Education, Children's Services and Skills (Ofsted) Common Inspection Framework has been revised to give more attention to English and mathematics.

Source: Kuczera M., S. Field and H. Windisch (2016), *Building Skills for All: A Review of England. Policy Insights from the Survey of Adult Skills*, www.oecd.org/edu/skills-beyond-school/building-skills-for-all-review-of-england.pdf.

References

The American Association of University Women (2015), *Solving the Equation: The Variables for Women's Success in Engineering and Computing*, www.aauw.org/research/solving-the-equation/.

Australian Government (2016), *Australian Education System*, www.studyinaustralia.gov.au/global/australian-education/education-system (accessed 10 October 2017).

The Australian Industry Group (2016), *Workforce Development Needs. Survey Report*, http://cdn.aigroup.com.au/Reports/2016/15396_skills_survey_report_mt_edits_2.pdf?_cldee=Z3JhaGFtLnR1cm5lckBhaWdyb3VwLmNvbS5hdQ%3d%3d&recipientid=contact-5622c0dde9fb4f51a93872c8a5920899-0019e63eeb76407394f57121ca91d9e3&esid=30016946-24c0-e611-80d0-0050568007a5.

Cook, H. (2015) "Christopher Pyne pushes for maths or science to be compulsory for year 11 and 12 students", *The Sydney Morning Herald*, 26 May 2015, www.smh.com.au/federal-politics/political-news/christopher-pyne-pushes-for-maths-or-science-to-be-compulsory-for-year-11-and-12-students-20150525-gh9kjv.html.

Education and Employers Taskforce (2016), *Inspiring the Future*, www.educationandemployers.org/programmes/inspiring-the-future/.

Finnie, R. and Frenette, M. (2003), "Earning differences by major field of study: evidence from three cohorts of recent Canadian graduates", *Economics of Education Review*, Vol. 22/2, pp. 179-192.

Kennedy, J. P. T. Lyons and F. Quinn (2014), "The continuing decline of science and mathematics enrolments in Australian high schools", *Teaching Science,* Vol. 60/2, pp. 34-46.

Kuczera M., S. Field and H. Windisch (2016), *Building Skills for All: A Review of England. Policy Insights from the Survey of Adult Skills*, www.oecd.org/edu/skills-beyond-school/building-skills-for-all-review-of-england.pdf.

Lane, M. and G. Conlon (2016), "The impact of literacy, numeracy and computer skills on earnings and employment outcomes", *OECD Education Working Papers*, No. 129, OECD Publishing, Paris, http://dx.doi.org/10.1787/5jm2cv4t4gzs-en.

OECD (2016), *Education at a Glance 2016: OECD Indicators*, OECD Publishing, Paris, http://dx.doi.org/10.1787/eag-2016-en.

OECD (2014), *PISA 2012 Results: What Students Know and Can Do* (Volume I, Revised edition, February 2014): Student Performance in Mathematics, Reading and Science, OECD Publishing, Paris, http://dx.doi.org/10.1787/9789264208780-en.

OECD (2013), *Skills Outlook 2013: First Results from the Survey of Adult Skills*, OECD Publishing, Paris, http://dx.doi.org/10.1787/9789264204256-en.

OECD (2012), *Survey of Adult Skills (PIAAC)*, Database 2012, www.oecd.org/site/piaac/publicdataandanalysis.htm.

OECD (2011), *Report on the Gender Initiative: Gender Equality in Education, Employment and Entrepreneurship*, www.oecd.org/education/48111145.pdf.

OECD (2006), PISA database 2006, www.oecd.org/pisa/pisaproducts/database-pisa2006.htm.

Paccagnella, M. (2016), "Age, ageing and skills: Results from the Survey of Adult Skills", *OECD Education Working Papers*, No. 132, OECD Publishing, Paris, http://dx.doi.org/10.1787/5jm0q1n38lvc-en.

Phillips, N. (2016), "20-year decline in year 12 science and maths participation, study finds", *The Sydney Morning Herald,* 6 October 2014, www.smh.com.au/technology/sci-tech/20year-decline-in-year-12-science-and-maths-participation-study-finds-20141006-10qvq2.html.

Chapter 4. Low-skilled adults in post-secondary vocational education and training (VET) in Australia

Some post-secondary vocational education and training (VET) students lack upper-secondary qualifications. Such students are much more likely to perform poorly in basic skills than their peers with higher levels of education. Women are also over-represented among students with low basic numeracy and literacy skills. These findings show that initiatives targeting specific categories of post-secondary VET students, such as those with few qualifications and students in specific fields of study could be particularly effective. This chapter also discusses the importance of addressing underperformance in basic skills as a part of post-secondary VET studies.

The statistical data for Israel are supplied by and are under the responsibility of the relevant Israeli authorities. The use of such data by the OECD is without prejudice to the status of the Golan Heights, East Jerusalem and Israeli settlements in the West Bank under the terms of international law.

Characteristics of low-skilled post-secondary VET graduates

Some post-secondary VET graduates lack basic skills

In Australia, around 16% of adults (16-65 year-olds) hold post-secondary qualifications, most of which are vocational (see Table 1.1 for classification of VET programmes). Some 15% of all post-secondary VET graduates lack basic numeracy or literacy skills (see Figure 4.1). While the percentage of post-secondary VET graduates with low skills in Australia is similar to the average of participating countries, it is above the share of low-skilled adults with equivalent qualifications in some other countries, such as Austria, Denmark, Germany and Sweden. Poor numeracy skills are more common among post-secondary VET graduates in Australia than poor literacy.

Figure 4.1. Low skilled among post-secondary VET graduates

16-65 year-olds, 2012

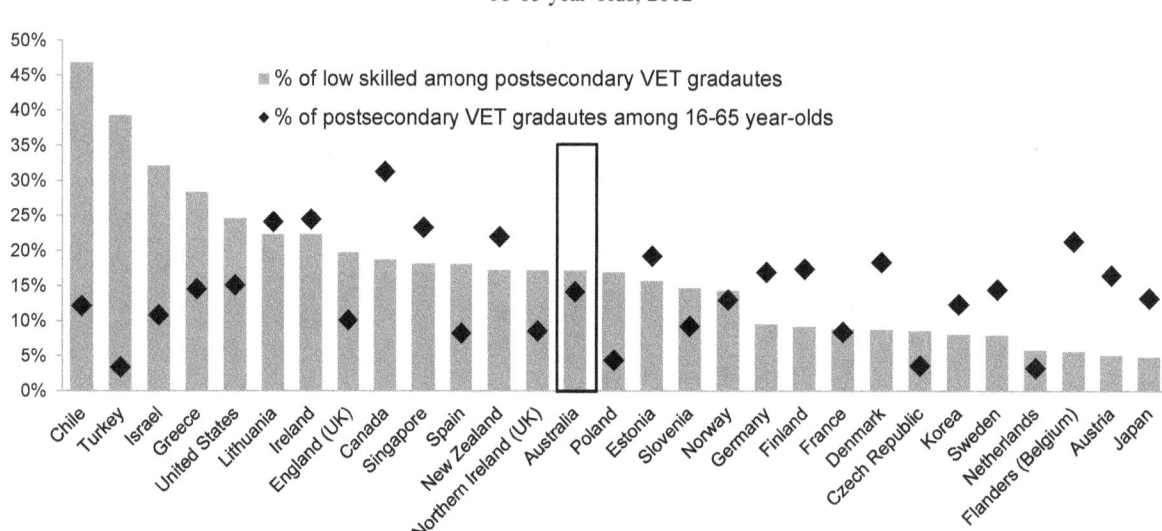

Note: Results for the Slovak Republic and Italy were not shown due to a small sample size. Foreign qualifications were excluded.
Source: OECD calculations based on OECD (2016a), *Survey of Adult Skills (PIAAC)* (Database 2012, 2015), www.oecd.org/site/piaac/publicdataandanalysis.htm.

StatLink http://dx.doi.org/10.1787/888933573544

Some post-secondary VET students lack basic skills

Around 17% of current post-secondary VET students have low basic skills (literacy or numeracy) (see Figure A A.3 in Annex A), with low numeracy being more common than low literacy. There is no difference in the share of low basic skills among students in Certificate IV and those studying for a higher post-secondary level qualification. The poor performance of these students shows that some individuals lack basic skills when they start a post-secondary VET programme. Some of these students may drop out or fail to graduate, others may improve their skills during their post-secondary studies. A large share of poorly performing recent graduates shows that for many students, the problem of basic skills is not resolved at the point of graduation (see Figure A A.3 in Annex A). Institutions providing these qualifications therefore do not sufficiently, or effectively, focus on remediating basic skills shortages among their students.

Recently, the Australian Government has introduced two initiatives to address these challenges. Foundation Skills Assessment Tool (FSAT), interactive online tool, was developed to identify and measure an individual's foundation skill levels. It can help training providers to address the individual needs of students. Recent changes to the Training and Education Training Package resulted in the inclusion of adult language, literacy and numeracy skills (the LLN unit) in the core units for the Certificate IV. The inclusion of the LLN unit in the Certificate IV was designed to provide VET practitioners with a greater understanding of the foundation skills required in their industry sectors.

There are large variations in the distribution of basic skills among current students

A relatively large gap between the best and the worst performers both in literacy and numeracy may indicate large variations in basic skills distribution across regions, institutions or fields of study (as indicated by the length of the bar in Figure 4.2). This is consistent with findings of a recent OECD report (OECD, 2016) that points to the varying quality of education and training among VET providers.

The consequences of being a low-skilled post-secondary VET graduate

While the majority of low-skilled graduates work, their situation in the labour market is more precarious

Some 72% of low-skilled post-secondary VET graduates were employed in 2012 (see Figure 4.3). While the employment rate of low-skilled graduates is relatively high, it is still 12 percentage points below the employment rate of all graduates with similar qualifications. The relatively high employment rate in this population may be explained by job-specific skills acquired in these programmes that are not tested in the Survey of Adult Skills (PIAAC) but rewarded in the labour market. It may also reflect a strong signalling value of post-secondary VET qualification, whereby employers use qualifications as signal of productivity and skills, independently of actual skills, or the fact that in 2012, demand for labour was high, with the overall unemployment rate around 5%. The situation of low-skilled adults in the labour market remains more precarious that that of highly skilled individuals, across all levels of educational attainment. For example, in Australia, low-skilled adults are more likely to work without a contract compared to adults with stronger skills. Post-secondary VET graduates with low skills could therefore be more vulnerable than their better skilled peers when economic and employment prospects worsen.

Figure 4.2. Skills distribution among current students
16-65 year-olds

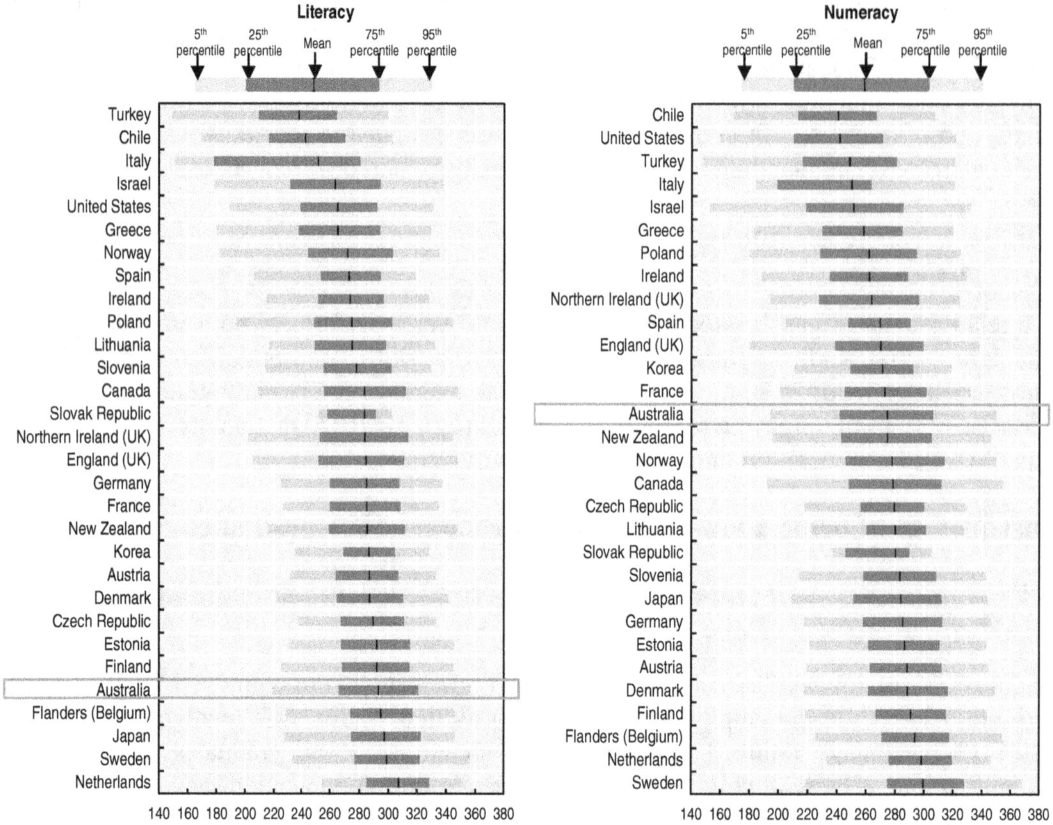

Source: OECD calculations based on OECD (2016a), *Survey of Adult Skills (PIAAC)* (Database 2012, 2015), www.oecd.org/site/piaac/publicdataandanalysis.htm.

StatLink http://dx.doi.org/10.1787/888933573563

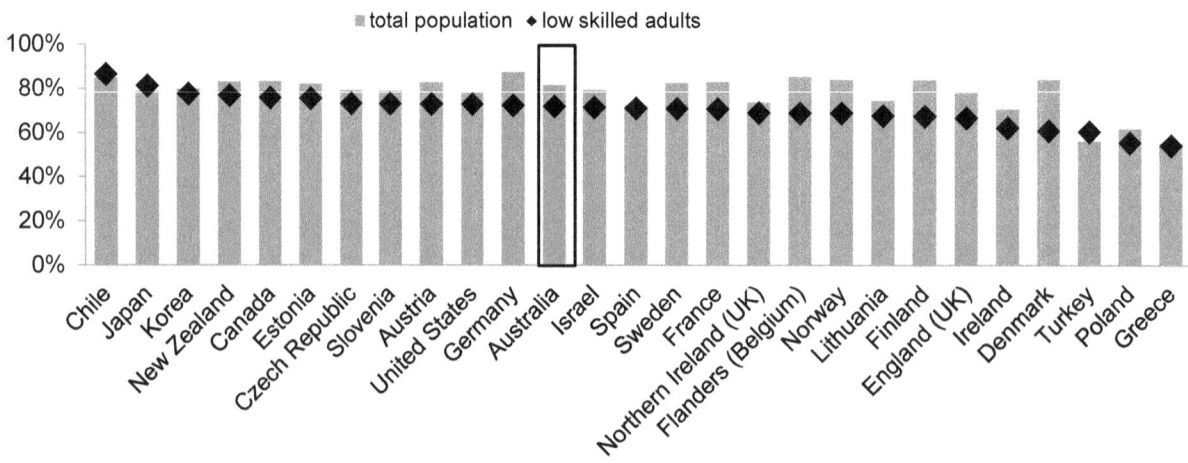

Figure 4.3. Employment rates among post-secondary VET graduates

16-65 year-olds, by skills

Source: OECD calculations based on OECD (2016a), *Survey of Adult Skills (PIAAC)* (Database 2012, 2015), www.oecd.org/site/piaac/publicdataandanalysis.htm.

StatLink http://dx.doi.org/10.1787/888933573582

Building Skills for All in Australia: Policy Insights from the Survey of Adult Skills © OECD 2017

Earnings of post-secondary VET graduates are associated with basic skills

In Australia, as in other countries, skills have a positive impact on wages. These findings also hold if the analysis is restricted only to those who graduated from post-secondary VET programmes, independently of gender, migration status, parental education, native language and age. This means that two identical people in terms of gender, migration status, native language and parental education, but with different levels of skills, will have different earnings. In Australia, a 50-point increase in numeracy skills, the number of points separating two different levels on numeracy scale, is associated with a 7% change in earnings (see Figure 4.4). Improvement in basic skills among current students may therefore increase returns to post-secondary VET qualifications. Reinforcing basic skills among post-secondary VET students and graduates would also have other advantages, such as reducing dropout from programmes and increasing the capacity of graduates to enter more highly skilled jobs and pursue further training and career development.

The majority of low-skilled post-secondary VET graduates are in occupations requiring mid or high-level skills

In comparison to highly skilled post-secondary VET graduates, those with low skills are less likely to work in jobs demanding high-level skills, such as managers and technicians, and more likely to work in occupations relying on mid-level skills, such as clerks, service workers and shop and market sales workers (for distribution of post-secondary VET graduates by skills and sectors see Figure A A.4 in Annex A). Nonetheless, 35% of low-skilled post-secondary VET graduates work in jobs requiring high-level skills. This may be due to skills other than numeracy and literacy that make low skilled post-secondary VET graduates suitable for these jobs. However, the high proportion of low-skilled individuals in these occupations could also be a sign of mismatch.

Figure 4.4. Effect of skills on earnings of post-secondary VET graduates

16-65 year-olds, 2012, percentage change in wages associated with an increase in numeracy by 50 points

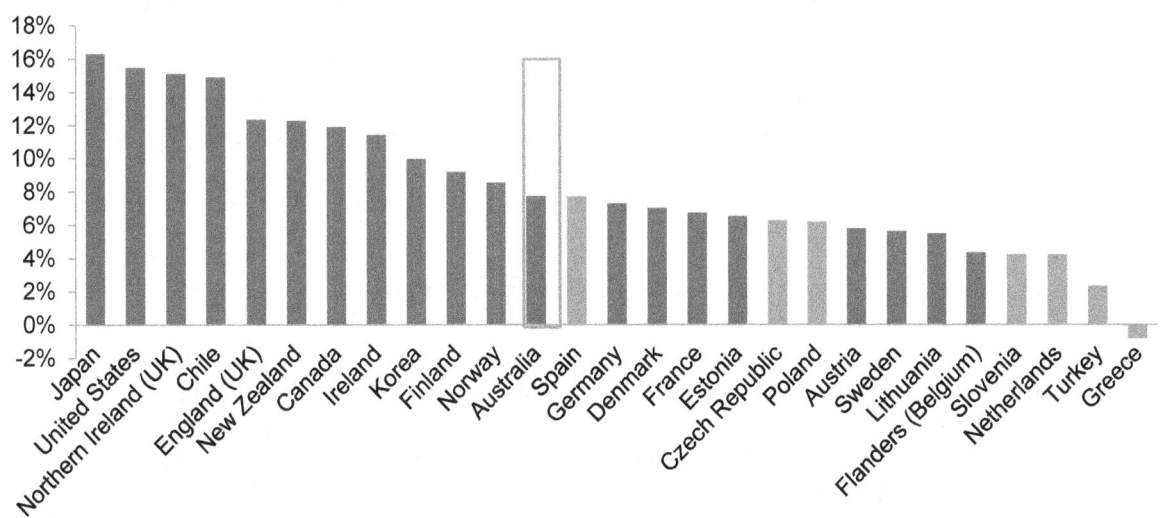

Note: Statistically significant results are marked in a darker tone. Adjusted for gender, migration status, native language and parental education.
Source: OECD calculations based on OECD (2016a), *Survey of Adult Skills (PIAAC)* (Database 2012, 2015), www.oecd.org/site/piaac/publicdataandanalysis.htm.

StatLink http://dx.doi.org/10.1787/888933573601

Recommendations: How to address the challenge of low basic skills in post-secondary VET

The remaining part of this section provides policy pointers on how to improve basic skills provision in post-secondary VET, while recognising that:

- Low basic skills among current students result from a mix of factors, such as previous education and labour market experience, use of skills at home, and personal and cohort characteristics.
- The skills of post-secondary VET graduates evolve after graduation, depending on the use of their skills in a work and out-of-work context.

Policy pointer 1: Identify students at risk of low basic skills and provide them with targeted initiatives

Australian post-secondary VET is inclusive and caters to a very diverse population: those preparing for a first career, those updating their skills while working and those who seek to validate skills acquired outside the education system. Post-secondary VET students also have very different educational experiences: 12 % have a qualification below upper-secondary level, 18% hold a university degree, nearly 40% have completed upper-secondary education, 24% already have a post-secondary qualification, and 6% studied abroad. While the inclusiveness of the post-secondary VET system is its strength, addressing the needs of a very diverse population can be challenging. An analysis of the association between age, gender, migration status, previous qualification and numeracy skills of post-secondary VET students shows that students whose highest qualification is below upper-secondary or upper-secondary VET are much more likely to perform poorly in numeracy than their peers with higher levels of education. Women are also over-represented among students with low basic numeracy skills. This could be due to the fact that women self-select themselves to the areas of study with lower requirements in numeracy. Being a migrant is not linked to numeracy performance. Age is positively associated with numeracy skills, but only among students with lower levels of education. This means that adults with low qualifications, and presumably low basic skills, might upgrade their skills after graduation through work. The findings of this analysis show that initiatives targeting specific categories of students, such as those with low and VET qualifications, and students in specific fields of study, could be particularly effective.

Policy pointer 2: Ensure post-secondary VET is good quality, with basic skills a quality criteria

Recent reforms have established a market in the provision of post-secondary VET, with public and private providers competing for public money. These reforms aimed to increase the number of VET participants, improve access to post-secondary education, and boost student choice. However, the reform also created a system that is complex and difficult to understand for students, and where quality varies greatly across providers. In the reporting year 2015-16, the Australian Skills Quality Authority (ASQA) found that in initial audit 82% of registered training providers did not fully comply with their standard of quality in training and assessment. After the rectification period which follows the initial audit report, 29% of training providers still did not fully comply. (Australian Skills Quality Authority, 2016). There is anecdotal evidence that private providers receiving public funding collude with students by offering them gifts and shopping vouchers for signing up for courses (e.g. Mitchell, 2016). A recent report by the Senate recognises the problems of abuse and low quality (Australian Senate, 2015) and recommends giving a larger role to ASQA to control and take action against training providers offering inadequate training to their students. Students with poor basic skills might be particularly concerned by the varying quality of provision across providers. Some institutions receiving per student funding may accept students with poor basic skills, with no intention or capacity to address this challenge.

Basic skills should be a quality criteria

While not all post-secondary VET jobs rely to the same extent on strong literacy or numeracy skills, it can be assumed that all require at least basic literacy and numeracy. Basic numeracy and literacy should therefore underpin all post-secondary VET qualifications. To address the quality challenge in VET, the Australian Government has recently revised standards for training providers (Registered Training Organisations). According to the new standards, the provider defines the amount of training regarding the existing skills, knowledge and experience of the learner. The provider should also have the capacity to provide educational and support services to the student to meet his or her needs (Australian Government, 2015). These standards could be interpreted in a way that strengthens the focus of VET providers on basic skills.

Example of successful initiatives

Box 4.1 describes the initiatives introduced in the United States to respond to the quality problem in post-secondary VET.

Box 4.1. How the United States responded to the quality challenge in post-secondary VET

The United States was facing, to some extent, similar challenges to Australia in post-secondary VET: quality in post-secondary VET was varied, private providers competed with public institutions for students and for federal money distributed through federal student loans, and students did not have access to full and accurate information on post-secondary VET choices and their outcomes. As a result, many students, typically from disadvantaged backgrounds, ended up with huge debts and education and training that was irrelevant to labour market needs. In response, the United States Department of Education established more stringent rules on VET post-secondary providers accessing federal dollars, making providers accountable for their labour market outcomes. For example the typical graduate's estimated annual loan must not exceed 20% of their discretionary income (what is left after basic necessities such as food and housing have been paid for) or 8% of total earnings. "Based on available data, the Department estimates that about 1 400 programmes serving 840 000 students – of whom 99% are at for-profit institutions – would not pass the accountability standards." (United States Department of Education, 2016).

An OECD report (Kuczera and Field, 2013) focusing on post-secondary VET in the United States lists a number of characteristics of good quality VET programmes that should be assured during the quality check. Similar criteria could be applied in Australia.

> Regarding basic skills, a good quality post-secondary VET programme should have:
>
> - Curricula reflecting the immediate requirements of employers, but also involving sufficient general and transferable skills to support career development; credentials with clear labour market recognition in the relevant industry sector.
> - Arrangements designed to provide targeted help to students who can benefit from the programme but have particular needs, such as numeracy and literacy weaknesses. (Kuczera and Field, 2013: 59).
>
> *Source*: Kuczera, M. and S. Field (2013), *A Skills beyond School Review of the United States*, http://dx.doi.org/10.1787/9789264202153-en; US Department of Education (2015), *Fact Sheet: Obama Administration Increases Accountability for Low-Performing For-Profit Institutions*, www.ed.gov/news/press-releases/fact-sheet-obama-administration-increases-accountability-low-performing-profit-institutions

Pointer 3: Encourage providers of post-secondary VET to address underperformance in basic skills

Remediating basic skills is difficult, but not impossible, as shown by the US example. In the United States, community colleges (public providers of post-secondary VET programmes) play an important role in providing qualifications for young adults, and in most states, access to the system is relatively easy and affordable, similar to Australia. Basic skills weaknesses among entrants are very common. To address this challenge, most public institutions provide remedial courses, although relatively few students referred for remediation end up completing the course. Faced with the failure of mainstream remedial education, US colleges and states have experimented with alternative, more targeted, but often also more expensive interventions, some of which have been successful. Providers of post-secondary VET qualifications in Australia, therefore, should be encouraged to address underperformance in basic skills more vigorously and effectively. For example, progress in basic skills made by students in post-secondary VET programmes could be one of the criteria of government funding for institutions offering the corresponding qualifications.

Examples of successful initiatives

Box 4.2 highlights an example of a funding incentive introduced in the state of Washington (United States) to improve college completion. While this initiative focuses primarily on student progression through the programme, similar incentives could be introduced to tackle low basic skills. It also describes the I-BEST model that provides basic skills in the context of learning vocational subjects.

> **Box 4.2. Innovative initiatives addressing poor basic skills in colleges in the United States**
>
> The Student Achievement Initiative (SAI) is a performance funding system for all community and technical colleges. It includes certificate and associate degrees (one and two-year programmes), apprenticeship retraining for workers, and a programme for adults without a high school diploma. Institutions are rewarded with additional funds if they record a positive change in the number of students that move from remedial to credit courses, complete specific credits, and successfully complete the degree. Colleges are evaluated based on the progress made relative to their own prior performance. As one official document states: "there are no targets, colleges compete with themselves rather than each other" (SBCTC, 2013). SAI does not affect the regular formula by which the state distributes funds among institutions.
>
> The model tracks student progress over time, from basic skills courses to the completion of a degree. It encourages institutions to measure the impact of tools designed to improve student progression. On this basis, institutions can identify and adjust their practices genuinely contributing to student progression. This focus on student progression and completion has increased attention on basic skills and remedial education, and had also led to stronger investment in student services (Jenkins et al., 2009).
>
> The evidence collected through systematic evaluation of SAI shows that the number of students in technical and community colleges reaching crucial progression points (momentum points) has been growing since its introduction. In particular, more students perform better in basic skills and are college ready. Over the same period, more students are enrolled in community and technical colleges, which contributes to the higher number of students progressing through the system. However, the achievement gains grew at a much faster rate than the number of students enrolled, which implies that better student achievement explains an important part of this improvement (SBCTC, 2013). There is also little evidence that colleges serving more at-risk, low-income students are penalised by the SAI funding (Belfield, 2012). The growth in student performance halted in 2011, which could be related to funding cuts in post-secondary education.
>
> I-BEST (the Integrated Basic Education and Skills Training) is an innovative blend of basic skills with vocational education and training. Often too few students in adult basic skills programmes upgrade their skills by transferring to post-secondary education. I-BEST was developed to improve entry rates to post-secondary career and technical education (CTE) in response to this challenge. Around 2% of basic skills students participated in I-BEST between 2006 and 2008 (Wachen et al., 2010). An I-BEST programme combines basic skills teaching and professional training. Occupational training yields college credits that contribute to a certificate degree. These CTE courses can only be provided in occupations in demand in the labour market and leading to well-paid jobs (Wachen et al., 2010). Combining basic skills with CTE content is facilitated by the availability of both types of programme at community and technical colleges (I-BEST programmes are available in every community and technical college in Washington State) (WTECB, 2013a). Individuals must score below a certain threshold on an adult skill test and qualify for adult basic education to participate in an I-BEST programme. I-BEST students tend to perform

better than non-participants and are more likely to have a high school or equivalent qualification.

In the I-BEST programme, a teacher of basic skills and a teacher of professional-technical subject jointly instruct in the same classroom with at least a 50% overlap of instructional time (SBCTC, 2012). This increases the cost of provision, and the state therefore funds I-BEST students at 1.75 times the normal per capita funding rate. From an individual point of view, I-BEST programmes are more expensive than adult basic education as students pay for the college-level portion of the I BEST programme. This may prevent some adults from participating, as many I-BEST students are from low-income families and cannot afford tuition in college-level classes (Wachen et al., 2010). Students can receive financial support from federal (Pell grant) and state sources (state need grant and opportunity grant), but as reported by Wachen et al., (2010), many students interested in I-BEST do not qualify for this aid. Proving eligibility for the financial aid can sometimes be complicated and deter students from applying.

A few studies measuring the impact of I-BEST found that I-BEST students earn more credits and are more likely to complete a degree than a comparable group of basic skill students not participating in the programme. Evidence on the link between participation in I-BEST and earnings is less conclusive, although this might be due to changing economic conditions and the United States and Washington State economy entering recession (Jenkins et al., 2010).

Source: SBCTC (2012), Integrated Basic Education and Skills Training (I-BEST), www.sbctc.edu/colleges-staff/programs-services/i-best/; Belfield C. (2012), "Washington State Student Achievement Initiative: Achievement Points Analysis for Academic Years 2007-2011", CCRC-HELP Student Achievement Initiative Policy Study; Jenkins D., T. Ellwein and K. Boswell (2009), Formative Evaluation of the Student Achievement Initiative Learning Year, Report to the Washington State Board for Community and Technical Colleges and College Spark Washington, CCRC; Wachen J., D. Jenkins and M. Van Noy (2010), How I-BEST Works: Findings from a Field Study of Washington State's Integrated Basic Education and Skills Training Program, CCRC, New York; Jenkins D., M. Zeidenberg and G. Kienzl (2010), "Educational outcomes of I-BEST, Washington State community and technical college system's integrated basic education and skills training program: Findings from a multivariate analysis", Working Paper No. 16, CCRC in Kuczera M. and S. Field (2013), Skills beyond School Review of the United States, http://dx.doi.org/10.1787/9789264202153-en.

References

Australian Government (2015), *Standards for Registered Training Organisations (RTOs) 2015*, Federal Register of Legislation, www.legislation.gov.au/Details/F2014L01377.

Australian Government, Department of Education and Training (2017), *Foundation Skills Assessment Tool*, www.education.gov.au/foundation-skills-assessment-tool (accessed 1 April 2017).

Australian Senate (2015), *Getting Our Money's Worth: The Operation, Regulation and Funding of Private Vocational Education and Training (VET) Providers in Australia*, Parliament House, Canberra. www.voced.edu.au/content/ngv%3A70322.

Australian Skills Quality Authority (2016), *Australian Skills Quality Authority. Annual Report 2015–16*, Commonwealth of Australia, www.asqa.gov.au/sites/g/files/net2166/f/ASQA_Annual_Report_2015-16.pdf.

Belfield C. (2012), "Washington State Student Achievement Initiative: Achievement Points Analysis for Academic Years 2007-2011", CCRC-HELP Student Achievement Initiative Policy Study

Jenkins D., T. Ellwein and K. Boswell (2009), *Formative Evaluation of the Student Achievement Initiative Learning Year*, Report to the Washington State Board for Community and Technical Colleges and College Spark Washington, CCRC.

Jenkins D., M. Zeidenberg and G. Kienzl (2010), "Educational outcomes of I-BEST, Washington State community and technical college system's integrated basic education and skills training program: Findings from a multivariate analysis", *Working Paper,* No. 16, CCRC in Kuczera M. and S. Field (2013), *Skills beyond School Review of the United States*, OECD Reviews of Vocational Education and Training, OECD publishing, Paris, http://dx.doi.org/10.1787/9789264202153-en.

Kuczera, M. and S. Field (2013), *A Skills beyond School Review of the United States*, OECD Publishing, Paris, http://dx.doi.org/10.1787/9789264202153-en.

Mitchell (2012), *From Unease to Alarm: Escalating Concerns about the Model of 'VET Reform' and Cutbacks to TAFE*, John Mitchell and Associates. www.jma.com.au/upload/pages/home/_jma_vet-reform-document.pdf.

OECD (2016), *Investing in Youth: Australia*, OECD Publishing, Paris, http://dx.doi.org/10.1787/9789264257498-en.

SBCTC (2012), *Integrated Basic Education and Skills Training (I-BEST)*, www.sbctc.edu/colleges-staff/programs-services/i-best/, (accessed February 2013).

US Department of Education (2016), *Fact Sheet: Obama Administration Increases Accountability for Low-Performing For-Profit Institutions*, www.ed.gov/news/press-releases/fact-sheet-obama-administration-increases-accountability-low-performing-profit-institutions. (accessed 7 June 2017).

Wachen J., D. Jenkins and M. Van Noy (2010), *How I-BEST Works: Findings from a Field Study of Washington State's Integrated Basic Education and Skills Training Program*, CCRC, New York.

Chapter 5. Many young low-skilled Australians are not in employment, education or training (NEET)

In Australia about 600 000 of 16-29 year-olds, were not in employment, education or training (NEET) in 2015. This chapter examines the issue of NEETs, particularly the link between NEET status and low skills. Young people who leave education and training early are more likely to become NEET. Typically, students who are at risk of dropping out early from school disengage gradually, and there are early signs that can be helpful in identifying these students. Apprenticeships, or traineeships, can be a powerful tool to engage disconnected youth, as they offer an opportunity to learn and connect to the world of work. Young 16-29 year-old Australian women are three times more likely to be NEET than men. This chapter also discusses the importance of adequate access to childcare facilities for young mothers.

The statistical data for Israel are supplied by and are under the responsibility of the relevant Israeli authorities. The use of such data by the OECD is without prejudice to the status of the Golan Heights, East Jerusalem and Israeli settlements in the West Bank under the terms of international law.

The NEET challenge

Some 600 000 young Australians are not in employment, education or training

In Australia, 580 000, or 12%, of 16-29 year-olds, were NEET in 2015 (for the definition of NEET see Box 5.1). While this is less than in OECD countries on average, it still represents a challenge for the country. NEETs include young people who are unemployed and those who are outside the labour market and not looking actively for a job. Australia, with more than two-thirds of NEETs not looking for employment, has a relatively high share of inactive NEETs in comparison to other OECD countries (OECD, 2016a). This represents a serious challenge, as these young people are particularly difficult to be reached by public policies. By drawing on data from the Survey of Adult Skills, a product of the OECD Programme for the International Assessment of Adult Competencies (PIAAC), this section will examine the issue of NEETs, particularly the link between the NEET status and low skills.

Box 5.1. The definition of NEET used in this report

Drawing on the Survey of Adult skills (PIAAC), NEET are defined as 16-29 year-olds who are neither employed nor in education at the time of the assessment, but who may have participated in education or training in the last 12 months prior to the Survey.

To check the validity of the adopted definition, the results reported from the Survey of Adult Skills (PIAAC) were compared with information on NEETs from other data sources, such as the Australian Census and the Survey of Education and Work (SEW). Overall, the results reported from the Survey of Adult Skills (PIAAC) are consistent with the data from other sources, even though there may be slight differences due to different definitions used.

Characteristics of NEETs

Young people with low skills are more likely to become NEET

In most countries, young people (16-29 year-olds) with low skills are more likely to become NEET. In Australia, nearly one-fourth of young adults with low skills neither work nor study (see Figure 5.1). In the population of NEETs, one-third lack basic skills. Inactive NEETs are more often low skilled than unemployed NEET, and therefore represent a particularly vulnerable group.

Important regional variations

According to the Survey of Adult Skills (PIAAC), young NEETs are more common in some regions of the country. While only 8% of 16-29 year-olds are NEET in the Australian Capital Territory, in South Australia 16% of the youth cohort are NEET, and in Tasmania 23%.

High NEET rates among Aboriginal and Torres Strait Islander peoples

NEET rates are more than three times higher for Aboriginal and Torres Strait Islander youth than for other Australians (OECD, 2016a). While ethnicity is closely related to the NEET problem, the Survey of Adult Skills is unable to further explore this association due to the small sample size.

Figure 5.1. Young people with low skills are more likely to become NEET

Share of NEETs in the total population of 16-29 year-olds and among 16-29 year-olds with low skills

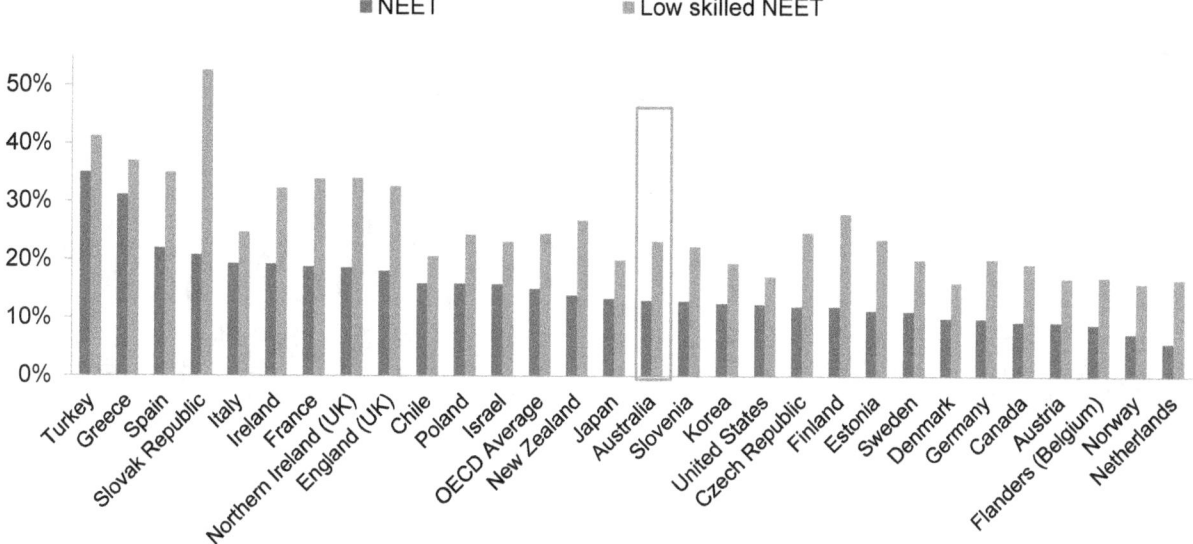

Source: OECD calculations based on OECD (2016a), *Survey of Adult Skills (PIAAC)* (Database 2012, 2015), www.oecd.org/site/piaac/publicdataandanalysis.htm.

StatLink http://dx.doi.org/10.1787/888933573620

Parental education level has a significant impact on becoming NEET

The OECD's Programme for International Student Assessment (PISA) evaluations show that youth from socio-economically disadvantaged backgrounds perform less well in school than children with more advantageous backgrounds. Several research studies argue that the inequalities developed in school tend to persist or widen later on in adult life, (e.g. Crawford, Macmillan, and Vignoles, 2015 on England). In line with these findings, the Survey of Adult Skills (PIAAC) shows that adults with a disadvantaged background (as measured by the level of parental education) are more likely to have low basic skills and perform less well in the labour market than those with well-educated parents (OECD, 2016a). They are also more at risk of becoming NEET. In Australia, adults whose parents did not complete upper-secondary education are twice as likely to become NEET than those whose parents attained tertiary level education (see Figure 5.2). This difference is, however, much smaller in Australia than in most participating countries, which indicates that factors other than parental education may have a stronger bearing on becoming NEET in Australia.

Many NEETs have low educational attainment

Almost 40% of Australian NEETs have qualifications below upper-secondary education (completed junior secondary school, certificate I or II qualification) compared to 22% of non NEETs in the same age group. One NEET in ten obtained certificate III as the highest qualification, and one in four completed senior secondary school.

Figure 5.2. Are those with less-educated parents more likely to become NEET?

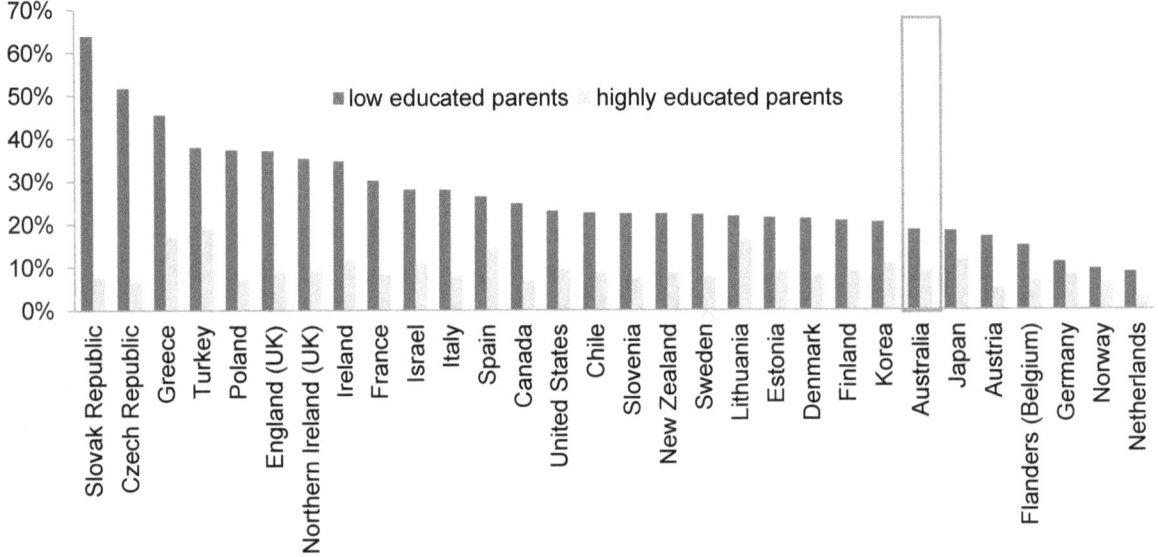

Share of NEETs among 16-65 year-olds whose parents did not complete upper-secondary education (low-educated parents) and those whose parents completed tertiary education (highly-educated parents)

Source: OECD calculations based on OECD (2016a), *Survey of Adult Skills (PIAAC)* (Database 2012, 2015), www.oecd.org/site/piaac/publicdataandanalysis.htm.

StatLink ᓚᘏᗢ http://dx.doi.org/10.1787/888933573639

Many NEETs have dropped out of school

Almost 45% of Australian NEET's are dropouts, which is above the average of 30% among participating countries, and similar to countries such as Norway, the Netherlands and the United States.

NEETs have lower non-cognitive skills

NEET's in Australia have lower levels of non-cognitive skills than non-NEET youth. The gap between NEETs and non-NEETs is significant for all of the big five personality traits (openness, extroversion, emotional stability, conscientiousness and agreeableness), and particularly large for openness to experience and conscientiousness.

Being a foreign born is not associated with being a NEET in Australia

In Australia, 16-29 year-old immigrants are as likely as natives to be NEET. This differs from most participating countries, where NEETs are over-represented among immigrants. In some countries, such as New Zealand and the United Kingdom, the situation is reversed: the native population is more likely to be NEET than immigrants.

There are more NEETs among women

In Australia, young 16-29 year-old women are three times more likely to be NEET than men. There are 13% of NEETs among young women, compared to 4% among men. As a result, the majority (70%) of 16-29 year-old NEETs are women. In nearly all participating countries, women are more likely to be NEETs than men, but in Australia, the share of women among NEETs is particularly high.

Figure 5.3. Non-NEET youth score higher for non-cognitive abilities than NEETs

Source: OECD (2016), *Investing in Youth: Australia*, Figure 2.3, http://dx.doi.org/10.1787/9789264257498-en.

StatLink http://dx.doi.org/10.1787/888933573658

Figure 5.4. Share of NEET among native born and immigrants

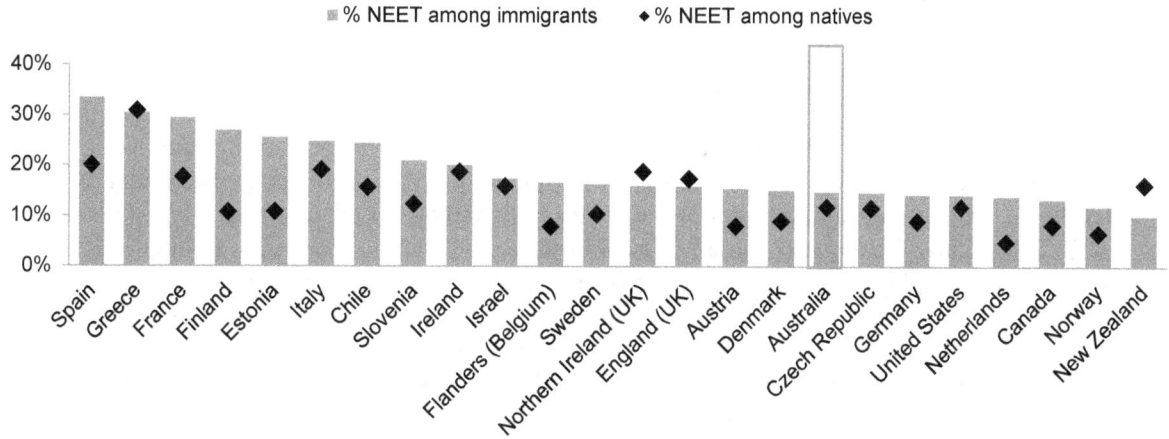

Source: OECD calculations based on OECD (2016a), *Survey of Adult Skills (PIAAC)* (Database 2012, 2015), www.oecd.org/site/piaac/publicdataandanalysis.htm.

StatLink http://dx.doi.org/10.1787/888933573677

Women with childcare responsibilities

The over-representation of women among young NEETs can be related to the fact that women more often take on childcare responsibilities: 64% of female NEETs are parents compared to 15% of men. Young women with children, especially those with low levels of education and training, are particularly at risk of being NEET in Australia.

Distilling the most important factors

Some factors are particularly decisive in becoming NEET, and some characteristics are correlated. For example, students with lower performance are more likely to dropout and stop education early on. The Survey of Adult Skills (PIAAC) helps to fine tune the analysis by looking simultaneously at associations between different factors and the likelihood of becoming NEET. Analysis taking into account characteristics such as numeracy skills, dropping out from education and training, years of education, gender, spoken language, migrant status and parental education shows that in Australia, gender is very strongly associated with the NEET status. This association is stronger in Australia than in all other countries, except Turkey. Speaking a language other than English and leaving education and training early are also risk factors in Australia.

The consequences of being NEET

Disconnection from the labour market has lasting consequences

By the age of 29, one in four NEETs had some paid work, compared to almost half of non-NEET Australians of the same age. Furthermore, only 33% of Australian NEETs are actively looking for a paid job, compared to almost 50% in the United States, the United Kingdom and Sweden, and 43% in New Zealand. This group is typically much harder to reach out to and more challenging to bring into employment. Limited work exposure and disconnection from the labour market among young people can have lasting consequences, as first experience in the labour market is important. Those who go through spells of joblessness at early stages of their careers tend to suffer from a "scarring effect", which leads to higher chances of unemployment and lower earnings later on in life than their peers with similar backgrounds and abilities (e.g. Bell and Blanchflower, 2011; Nilsen and Reiso, 2011). The longer the time spent as a NEET the more difficult the re-entry into education and working life.

Being low skilled and NEET is doubly disadvantageous

People acquire skills in different settings, such as education and training or through work. Young people who are low skilled and not working are doubly disadvantaged as they are excluded from two major institutions through which they could upgrade their skills. NEETs with low literacy and numeracy skills also face substantial hurdles to re-engage in education or employment. Many may not be able to immediately start vocational training or work due to poor basic skills and weak non-cognitive competencies. Low basic skills may also coincide with social or health problems, such as family problems, mental health, and substance abuse issues. These issues can be both a cause or a consequence of being NEET. The young person with such problems will require intensive assistance through social or health services while, and possibly before, participating in any form of training facilitating transition to employment.

NEETs report lower levels of trust and participation in volunteer activities

NEETs are less likely to take part in other aspects of social life. As seen in Chapter 1, the Survey of Adult Skills collects information on four non-economic outcomes, such as the level of trust in others; participation in associative, religious, political or charity activities (volunteering); the sense of being able to influence the political process (i.e. political efficacy); and self-assessed health conditions. For each of these non-economic outcomes, Australian disadvantaged youth reported lower levels of engagement than their more advantaged peers. NEETs are less likely to report high levels of trust (23% vs. 15% among non-NEETs) and almost half as likely to do volunteer work (26% vs. 40%).

NEETs are costly

An OECD study, *Society at a Glance 2016* (OECD, 2016b), estimated that the cost of NEETs in Australia in 2014 was around 1% of Australian GDP (see Figure 5.5). This cost includes the gross labour income (including social security contribution) that a NEET would generate had he or she worked. This estimate assumes that NEETs would receive a "low-wage", which is two-thirds of the median wage among youth of the same gender and age. The total cost of NEETs reflects both the NEET rates and wage levels. In Australia, relatively high wages drive the cost of NEETs up, despite the relatively low NEET rates. It is important to note that these estimates are an approximation. The cost can be overestimated if some people give up work to contribute to the well-being of their families and communities. However, the presented cost can also be underestimated as it does not include out-of-work benefits some NEETs receive, and the costs associated with higher rates of health problems and criminality among NEETs.

Figure 5.5. NEET costs are significant in many OECD countries

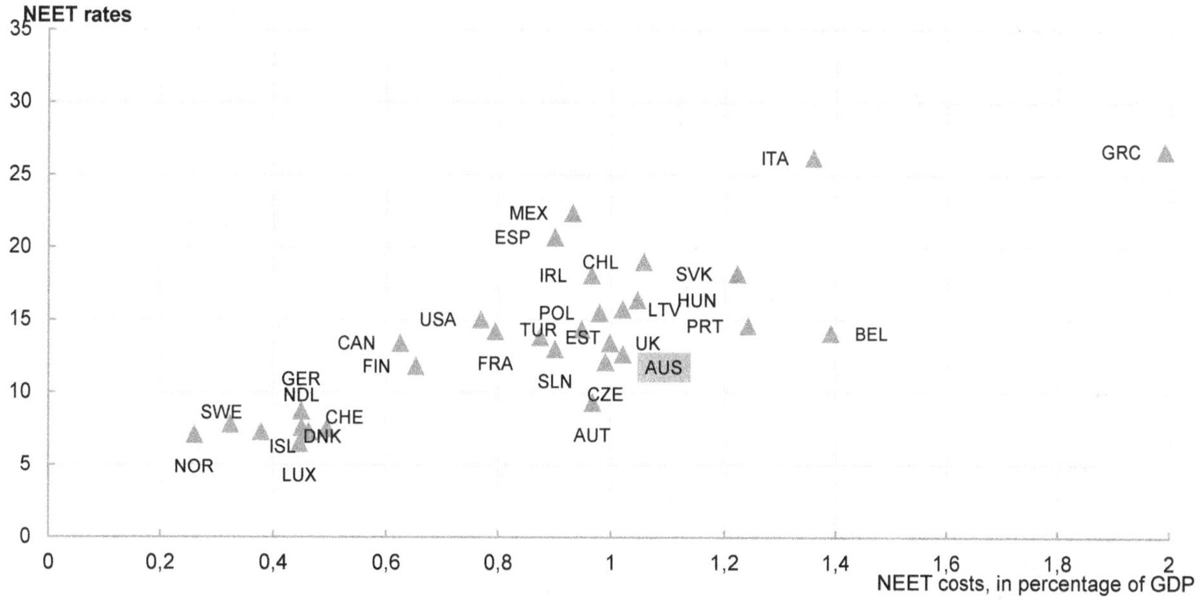

Source: OECD (2016), *Society at a Glance 2016: OECD Social Indicators*, http://dx.doi.org/10.1787/9789264261488-en.

StatLink http://dx.doi.org/10.1787/888933573696

Recommendations: How to tackle the NEET challenge

Policy pointer 1: Reach out to disconnected youth and prevent dropout from early stages of education

Reaching out to young people at risk who are still in school is easier than targeting those who have already left school and are loosely connected to the labour market. Young people who left education and training early are more likely to become NEET. Typically, students who are at risk of dropping out early from school disengage gradually, and there are early signs that can be helpful in identifying these students (see for example Lyche, 2010).

Examples of successful initiatives

Many countries have developed specific policies to increase the completion of at least upper-secondary education among young people. These involve early identification and follow up of individuals at risk.

Box 5.2. How to increase completion

Follow-up services in Norway

In response to high dropout rates among young people, Norway has set up a specific policy based on early identification and prevention. In Norway, all county (local) authorities are legally obliged to follow up on NEETs aged 16 to 21, they should also prevent youth at risk from dropping out of school. Since 1994, country services following up on NEETs reach out to all young people who are not in employment or education. They provide them with counselling and connect them with the local employment and welfare office. They also co-ordinate activities directed at NEETs that are provided by other agencies. The approach towards NEETs is tailored to the needs of individuals and combines elements of work exposure and of schooling delivered by education institutions. In Oslo, for instance, the follow-up service receives a list of dropouts four times per year, and there are 110 counsellors located directly in Oslo's schools (both lower-and upper-secondary) (OECD, 2016a).

Municipal Youth Guidance Centres in Denmark

These centres are responsible for monitoring 15-24 year-olds' transition from lower to upper-secondary school, and for following up on those who drop out of school. There are 45 Youth Guidance Centers covering 98 municipalities. Guidance activities include individual and group guidance sessions, as well as introductory courses and bridge-building programmes to give young people a clearer idea of their options. These bridge-building programmes combine individual counselling and teaching and last for 1-4 weeks. Counsellors prepare an education plan jointly with the pupils and their parents to ensure a smooth transition into upper-secondary education and employment. Those aged 15-17 are a special target group. In case of school non-attendance, counsellors have to get in touch with the youth's parents within five days of being notified by the school, and youth must be able to begin an activity within 30 days. The offered activity should be agreed upon by the youth, their parents and the counsellor, but young people may still reject the offer. In fulfilling its tasks, the Youth Guidance Centers are obliged to co-operate closely with the educational institutions and the municipal job centre for those aged 18 and above (OECD, 2016a).

Case management in Switzerland

The Swiss case management system is designed to support students who are at risk of dropping out during the transition from lower to upper-secondary education, and as a result leaving school without a secondary qualification. It was created in 2006 to help increase the number of students with a secondary qualification from 89% to 95% by 2015. It aims to co-ordinate different actors and institutions involved in the support of at risk-students and can be implemented during the phase of professional orientation at the end of lower-secondary school, during the transition phase from lower to upper-secondary schools, or during basic vocational education before a post-compulsory qualification is obtained.

> Case management is preventive rather than reactive in nature. Students at risk are first identified and their development monitored. Identification takes place at 7th and 8th grade in compulsory school, or later if students cannot find an apprenticeship or dropout of an apprenticeship or school-based VET course. A network of bodies (the case managers) is then mobilised to support the student in different tasks leading up to a full post-compulsory qualification.
>
> Support is tailor-made to individual needs, but can include help in choosing a pathway or finding an apprenticeship place upon finishing compulsory education, in getting back to education after dropout, as well as a range of additional support measures for young people with more general educational and social problems. The duration of case management is variable and depends on individual needs. The VET Offices in the Cantons (Berufsbildungsämter) have been responsible for the implementation of case management since 2008. They had to develop a concrete project proposal for approval by the federal government (Bundesamt für Berufsbildung und Technologie, BBT), who fund the initiative and are regularly monitored.
>
> *Source*: BBT (Bundesamt für Berufsbildung und Technologie) (2007), *Case Management*, Grundsätze und Umsetzung in den Kantonen, BBT, Bern.

A systematic approach that involves the identification and follow up of youth at risk is currently missing in Australia. One OECD (OECD, 2016a) study points to the fact that the current approach is fragmented as schools do not have to co-operate with social and healthcare providers. The role of local authorities in preventing dropout could also be reinforced. Currently, local authorities have no obligation to offer alternative options to school leavers or to follow up on those who left.

Policy pointer 2: Use pre-apprenticeships to help NEETs re-enter education and training and to find employment

Apprenticeships, or traineeships, can be a powerful tool to engage disconnected youth, as they offer an opportunity to learn and connect to the world of work. However, those most in need are likely to struggle to find and successfully complete an apprenticeship. Various initiatives that facilitate the transition from joblessness to training, or that provide a bridge between schools and apprenticeships, can be used to better prepare young people for their apprenticeship. These initiatives are called pre-apprenticeships.

Pre-apprenticeship programmes aim to develop skills that enable young people to find and successfully complete a work-based learning opportunity. They typically target the following skills:

- General academic skills, in particular literacy and numeracy instruction, and sometimes foreign language training.
- Vocational skills. In some programmes the focus is on career exploration, and participants learn about various occupations, and in others, participants develop skills related to a particular industry or apprenticeship occupation.
- Soft skills, covering both skills that young people need to find and be selected for a work-based learning opportunity (e.g. job search, CV writing and interview skills), as well as skills needed to succeed in a workplace (e.g. time-keeping, teamwork, resilience).

Australia has extensive experience with pre-apprenticeship programmes (such as the Kickstart Programme, Australian Access Programme, Group Training in Trades Programmes) that target young people who are already or run the risk of becoming NEET. However, the evidence on their effectiveness is mixed. Many initiatives did not meet their targets, and outcomes varied across states and territories. These two issues are further discussed below.

How to evaluate pre-apprenticeships?

Pre-apprenticeship programmes tend to be costly, and an important challenge is to identify which approaches work best. Various challenges arise in obtaining solid evaluation evidence on programmes that provide a bridge into apprenticeships (see Kis, 2016):

1. Within each country, state or region, the programmes offered tend to vary considerably in terms of content, duration, funding and mode of delivery. This means that average results may inadequately capture the quality of individual programmes.
2. Indicators, such as transition rate into apprenticeship or subsequent apprenticeship completion, need to be interpreted against the counterfactual: what would have happened to the youth had they not participated in a pre-apprenticeship? However, this is very difficult to measure, as young people who enter pre-apprenticeships tend to be more disadvantaged and have weaker skills than those who enter other education or training programmes or employment at the same age.
3. Various outcome measures could be envisaged, such as transition into apprenticeship, other education or training programme, or employment. However, a participant not entering an apprenticeship is necessarily a negative outcome, especially if the aim of the programme is to allow young people to test out whether an occupation suits them.
4. The costs and benefits of these programmes need to be compared with those of alternative scenarios (e.g. higher chance of reliance on unemployment benefits).

Co-ordination across various stakeholders and administrative levels is key for effective pre-apprenticeships

Programmes that create a bridge into apprenticeships are often at the intersection of education, employment and social policy. Diverse stakeholders may be involved in the funding, regulation and delivery of programmes, including federal and state level authorities, local authorities, and private entities (e.g. associations, foundations). One challenge associated with the diversity of programmes and actors involved is that provision is sometimes fragmented and leads to a confusing variety of isolated measures. In response to this challenge, Germany provided federal funding between 2008 and 2013 to an initiative to improve the co-ordination of transition offers at the regional level (*Perspektive Berufsabschluss - Regionales Übergangsmanagement*). This initiative included implementation strategies regarding networking, transparency of provision, parental involvement, and school/company co-operation (Aram et al., 2014). In addition, the "Educational chains" (*Bildungsketten*) initiative, launched in 2010, encourages a coherent and structured approach in career orientation and in the transition system (Kis, 2016).

Policy pointer 3: Improve access to childcare facilities for young mothers

Young women in Australia are much more likely to become NEET than young men. In Australia, this association is one of the highest among countries participating in the Survey, which signals the level of importance of the problem.

An analysis of various factors associated with being NEET among women used the Survey of Adult Skills to show that young women with children are more likely to become NEET in Australia. The majority of inactive young women mention flexibility in the workplace (including the ability to work part-time, to work from home, and flexibility in arranging working hours) as one of the key requirements for labour force participation. This is very likely related to their childcare responsibilities and the desire to combine childcare and work responsibilities. Australia's relatively high childcare costs also contribute to the very high NEET rates among young mothers with young children. More than half of young inactive women report that more childcare places, which are less expensive, would encourage them to work or search for a job (OECD, 2016a).

In order to help NEETs with children, particularly women, to enter the labour market or facilitate a return to education and training, childcare should be easy to access and costs should be kept at an affordable level. Several OECD countries offer good examples. Denmark operates a system whereby municipalities are obliged to offer all children older than six months a place in publicly subsidised childcare. In Sweden, municipalities must provide at least 15 hours of childcare per week to children over one. This obligation rises to full-time hours in cases where both parents are employed or in education. Other countries provide additional support for single parents, with Iceland (specifically Reykjavik) providing reduced childcare fees, and Belgium (Flemish Community) providing priority access to childcare services for lone parents.

References

Bell, D. and D. Blanchflower (2011), "Young people and the Great Recession", *Oxford Review of Economic Policy*, Vol. 27/2, pp. 241–67, https://doi.org/10.1093/oxrep/grr011.

Bundesamt für Berufsbildung und Technologie (2007), *Case Management*, Grundsätze und Umsetzung in den Kantonen, BBT, Bern.

Crawford, C., L. Macmillan and A. Vignoles (2015), "When and why do initially high attaining poor children fall behind?", *CASE - Social Policy in a Cold Climate Working Paper 20*, Centre for Analysis of Social Exclusion, LSE, https://ideas.repec.org/p/cep/spccwp/20.html.

Kis, V. (2016), "Work-based learning for youth at risk: Getting employers on board", *OECD Education Working Papers*, No. 150, OECD Publishing, Paris, http://dx.doi.org/10.1787/5e122a91-en.

Lyche, C. (2010), "Taking on the completion challenge: A literature review on policies to prevent dropout and early school leaving", *OECD Education Working Papers*, No. 53. OECD Publishing, Paris, http://dx.doi.org/10.1787/5km4m2t59cmr-en.

Nilsen, Ø. and K. Reiso (2011), "Scarring effects of unemployment", *IZA Discussion Paper 6198*, Institute for the Study of Labor (IZA), https://ideas.repec.org/p/iza/izadps/dp6198.html.

OECD (2016a), *Investing in Youth: Australia*, OECD Publishing, Paris, http://dx.doi.org/10.1787/9789264257498-en.

OECD (2016b), *Society at a Glance 2016: OECD Social Indicators*, OECD Publishing, Paris, http://dx.doi.org/10.1787/9789264261488-en.

Annex A. Key figures on adult skills in Australia versus other countries

Figure A A.1. Literacy proficiency and positive social outcomes

Adjusted difference between the percentage of adults with high proficiency (Levels 4 and 5) and the percentage of adults with low proficiency who reported high levels of trust and political efficacy, good to excellent health, or participating in volunteer activities

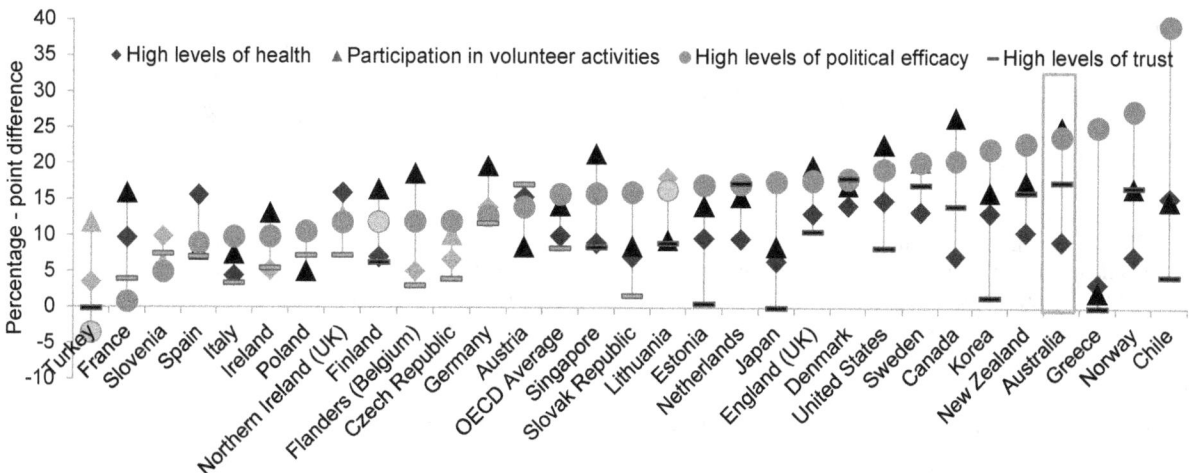

Note: Statistically significant differences are marked in a darker tone. Adjusted differences are based on a regression model and take account of differences associated with the following variables: age, gender, education, immigrant and language background and parents' educational attainment.

Source: Adapted from OECD (2016a), *Skills Matter: Further Results from the Survey of Adult Skills*, http://dx.doi.org/10.1787/9789264258051-en.

StatLink http://dx.doi.org/10.1787/888933573715

The statistical data for Israel are supplied by and are under the responsibility of the relevant Israeli authorities. The use of such data by the OECD is without prejudice to the status of the Golan Heights, East Jerusalem and Israeli settlements in the West Bank under the terms of international law.

Figure A A.2. **Percentage of first and second-generation migrants that have low basic skills (below Level 2 in literacy or/and numeracy) in comparison with the native-born**

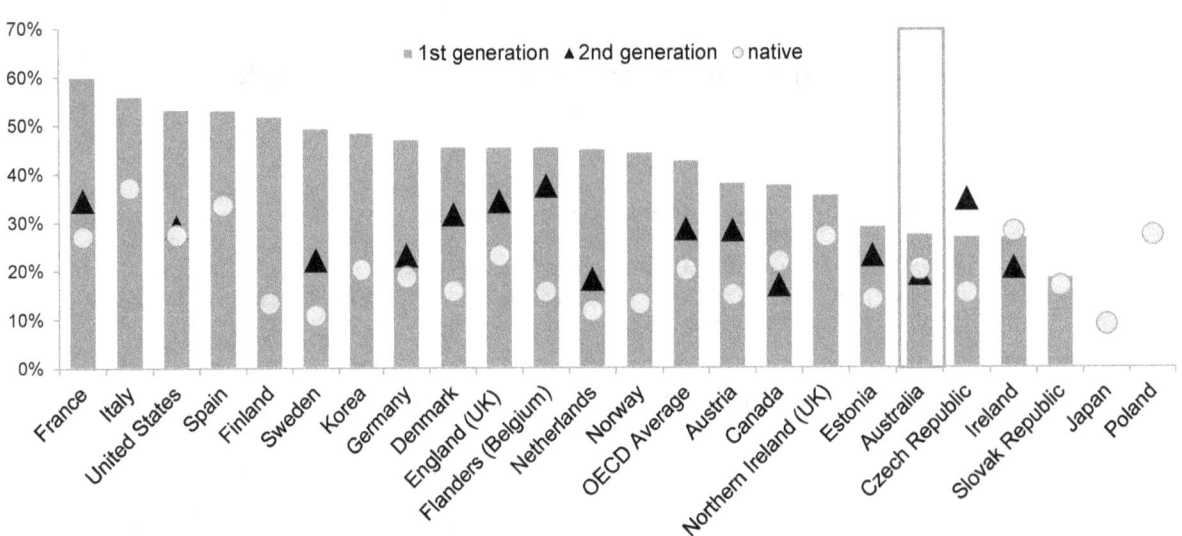

Note: First-generation immigrants: born abroad and with at least one parent born abroad), second-generation immigrants: born in Australia but both parents were born abroad), natives: born in Australia and both parents born in Australia.
Source: OECD calculations based on OECD (2016a), *Survey of Adult Skills (PIAAC)* (Database 2012, 2015), www.oecd.org/site/piaac/publicdataandanalysis.htm.

StatLink http://dx.doi.org/10.1787/888933573734

Figure A A.3. **Students and recently graduated students from post-secondary VET who lack basic skills**

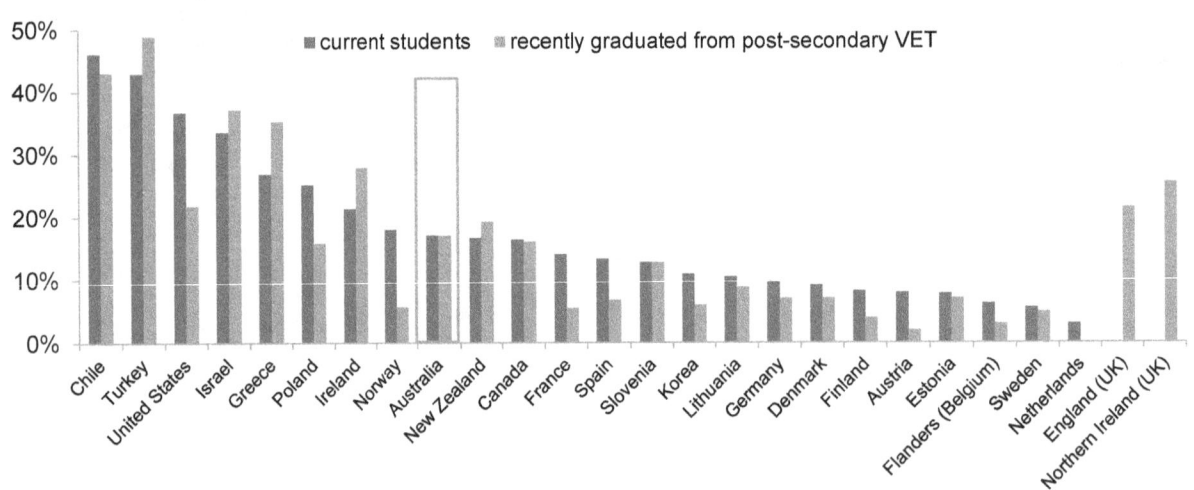

Source: OECD calculations based on OECD (2016a), *Survey of Adult Skills (PIAAC)* (Database 2012, 2015), www.oecd.org/site/piaac/publicdataandanalysis.htm.

StatLink http://dx.doi.org/10.1787/888933573753

Figure A A.4. In which sectors do post-secondary VET graduates work?

16-65 year-olds

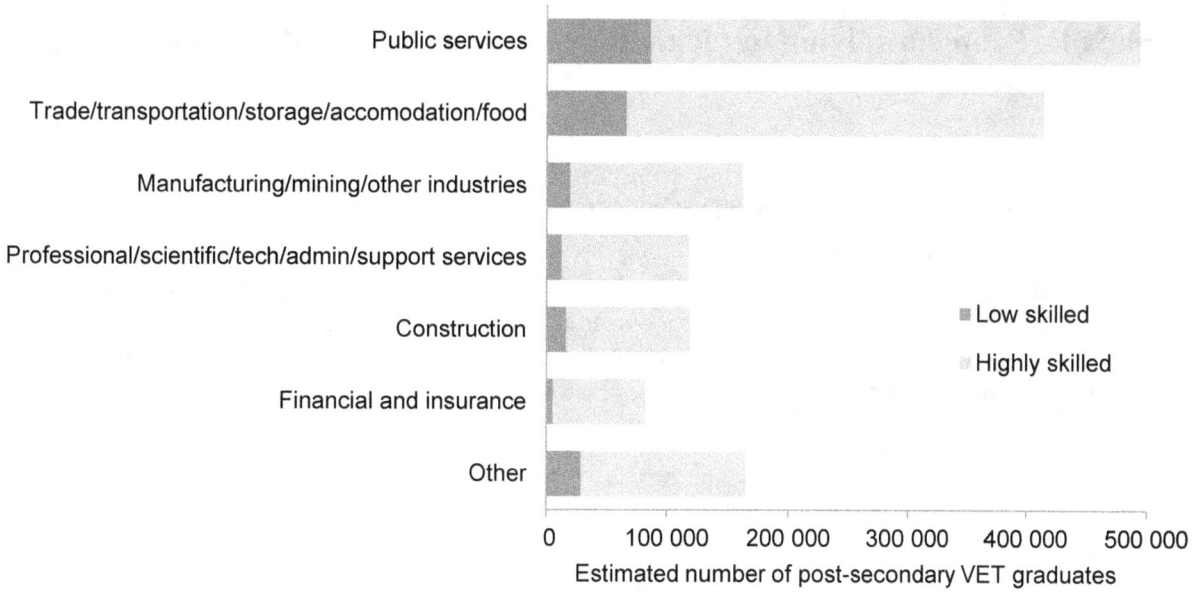

Source: OECD calculations based on OECD (2016a), *Survey of Adult Skills (PIAAC)* (Database 2012, 2015), www.oecd.org/site/piaac/publicdataandanalysis.htm.

StatLink http://dx.doi.org/10.1787/888933573772

References

OECD (2016a), *Skills Matter: Further Results from the Survey of Adult Skills*, OECD Publishing, Paris, http://dx.doi.org/10.1787/9789264258051-en.

OECD (2016b), *Survey of Adult Skills (PIAAC)* (Database 2012, 2015), www.oecd.org/site/piaac/publicdataandanalysis.htm.

Annex B. Problem solving in technology-rich environments – Sample items

> **Box B B.1. Sample task in problem solving in technology-rich environments**
>
> An example of a problem-solving item is provided below. This item involves a scenario in which the respondent assumes the role of a job-seeker. Respondents access and evaluate information relating to job search in a simulated web environment. This environment includes tools and functionalities similar to those found in real-life applications. Users are able to:
>
> - Click on links on both the results page and associated web pages.
> - Navigate, using the back and forward arrows or the Home icon.
> - Bookmark web pages and view or change those bookmarks.
>
>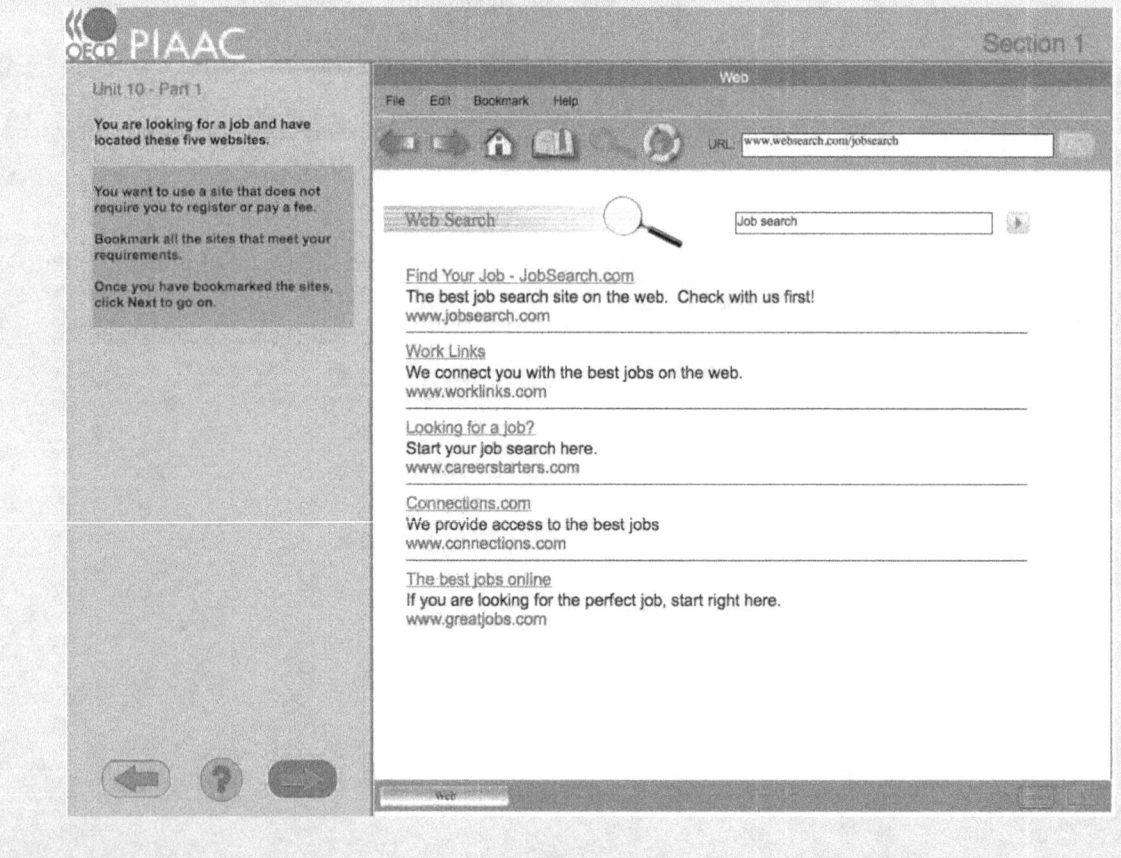

The first stimulus accessed by respondents is the results page of the search-engine application, which lists five employment agency websites. To complete the task successfully, respondents have to search through the pages of the listed websites to identify whether registration or the payment of a fee is required in order to gain further information about available jobs. Respondents can click on the links on the search page to be directed to the websites identified. For example, by clicking on the "Work Links" link, the respondent is directed to the home page of "Work Links".

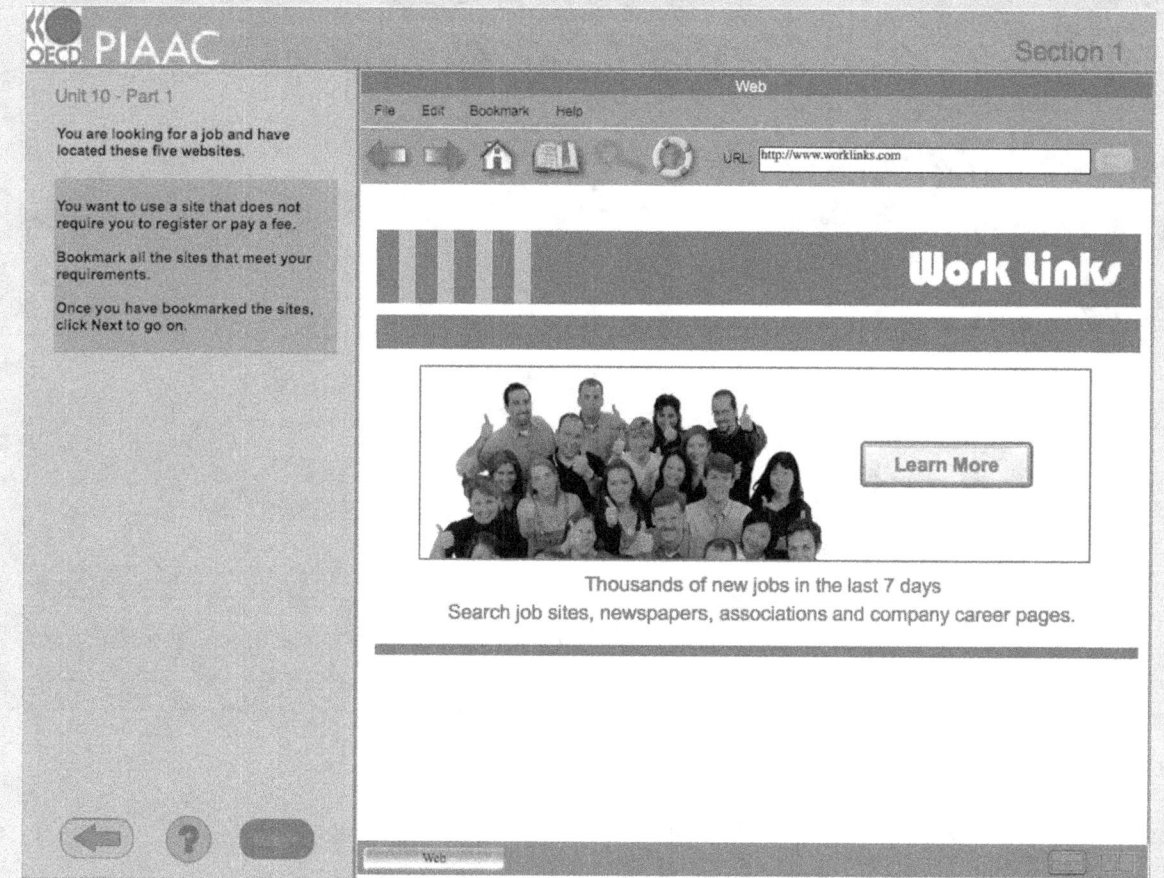

In order to discover whether access to the information on available jobs requires registration with the organisation or payment of a fee, the respondent must click the "Learn More" button which opens the following page. The respondent must then return to the search results page to continue evaluating the sites in terms of the specified criteria, using the back arrows without bookmarking the page (correct answer) or having bookmarked the page (incorrect answer).

Annex B. Problem solving in technology-rich environments – Sample items

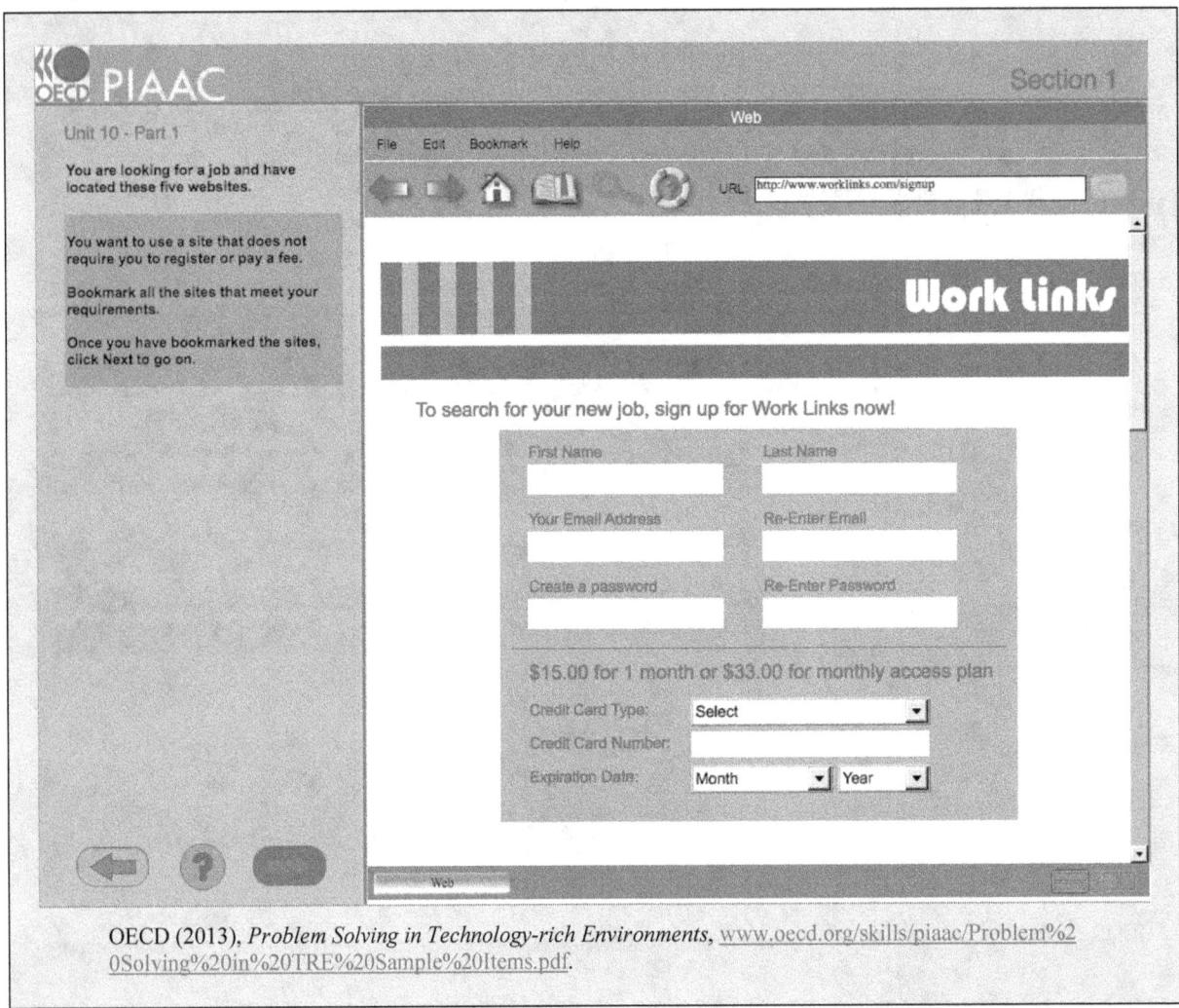

OECD (2013), *Problem Solving in Technology-rich Environments*, www.oecd.org/skills/piaac/Problem%20Solving%20in%20TRE%20Sample%20Items.pdf.

References

OECD (2013), *Problem Solving in Technology rich Environments*, www.oecd.org/skills/piaac/Problem%20Solving%20in%20TRE%20Sample%20Items.pdf.

ORGANISATION FOR ECONOMIC CO-OPERATION AND DEVELOPMENT

The OECD is a unique forum where governments work together to address the economic, social and environmental challenges of globalisation. The OECD is also at the forefront of efforts to understand and to help governments respond to new developments and concerns, such as corporate governance, the information economy and the challenges of an ageing population. The Organisation provides a setting where governments can compare policy experiences, seek answers to common problems, identify good practice and work to co-ordinate domestic and international policies.

The OECD member countries are: Australia, Austria, Belgium, Canada, Chile, the Czech Republic, Denmark, Estonia, Finland, France, Germany, Greece, Hungary, Iceland, Ireland, Israel, Italy, Japan, Korea, Latvia, Luxembourg, Mexico, the Netherlands, New Zealand, Norway, Poland, Portugal, the Slovak Republic, Slovenia, Spain, Sweden, Switzerland, Turkey, the United Kingdom and the United States. The European Union takes part in the work of the OECD.

OECD Publishing disseminates widely the results of the Organisation's statistics gathering and research on economic, social and environmental issues, as well as the conventions, guidelines and standards agreed by its members.

www.ingramcontent.com/pod-product-compliance
Lightning Source LLC
Chambersburg PA
CBHW082354220526
45470CB00008B/2745